Discover the
City of London Churches
A Walkers' Guide

by

John Barron & Alexandra Moore
Illustrated by Prue Gerrard

Foreword by
Sir Edward George
Governor of the Bank of England

Message by
The Rt Hon Rt Revd Richard Chartres
The Bishop of London

Barron and Moore
Winchester
2003

First published in 1998 as City of London Churches.
Second edition 2003 as
Discover the City of London Churches.
Barron and Moore,
9 Bartholomew Close,
Winchester, Hampshire SO23 7DL.

ISBN 0-9532798-2-0

Design, layout & typesetting by John Barron.
Set in Baskerville.

Printed in the United Kingdom by
Print on Demand, Antony Rowe Ltd. Eastbourne.

Dedicated to Paul Nicholas

Contents

Acknowledgements

Although acknowledgements are supposed to be best, like wine, on the dry side, it is not possible for us to follow this rule where our two friends, Peter Gerrard and Tom Spiers, are concerned. The debt of gratitude we owe them, for their continued help and interest in the book, is enormous and impossible to repay. Our thanks are also due to John Fisher and Jeremy Smith, of the Guildhall Library. Their unfailing help in our research, encouragement and interest in the book were invaluable. In Keith Ellis we were fortunate to find not only a superb photographer, but someone whose love of the City churches was as great as our own. Lastly, we would like to thank all the incumbents of City churches and their officers for their assistance and patience in answering questions.

Credits

For generously granting permission to use reproductions of their work, we thank the following.

Guildhall Library, Corporation of London.
Front and back covers: London by Johann Baptist Homann 1730
Back covers: London by Nicholas John Visscher
Page no.13.

Keith Ellis, ARPS.
Page nos. 8, 17, 36, 43, 44, 63, 80, 85, 88, 103

Max du Bois, BA (Hons.), FRGS.
Page nos. 54, 61, 91, 97, 101
Terence Dalley
Page no. 13
Westminster College, Fulton, Missouri, USA.
Page nos. 73,74

John Barron
All other photographs.

Quotations from John Stow, A Survey of London. Edited by C L Kingsford (1971) by permission of Oxford University Press.

Quotations from Diaries of Samuel Pepys,
by permission of Harper Collins Publishers Ltd.

Foreword

In spite of the ravages of the Great Fire, the Blitz and other depredations, a very large number of the City's churches have survived. This ecclesiastical heritage represents just one of London's hidden assets and one that through this book we can all appreciate more. They not only form an integral part of the colossal historical and cultural mosaic preserved in modern London, but also provide havens of tranquillity and spiritual sanctuary in the midst of the pressure, bustle and hurry of one of the world's largest financial centres. And, they are proof that the life of the City is deeply rooted in a sense of community, and bound together by institutions which reflect both its long heritage and its thriving modern face.

The authors are to be commended for providing a guide to the City's churches, which will be a valuable aid both to walkers who wish to see the churches at first hand, and for those who want a reference source of useful facts, and a collection of attractive illustrations.

Sir Edward George

Message from The Bishop of London
The Rt Hon & Rt Revd Richard Chartres DD FSA

A visit to any of the City's churches is an invitation to resist the tyranny of the momentary in order to dwell on what is enduring. For this to happen, however, some preparation is necessary. There is very little point in tearing round on an efficiently organised tour simply to take in some of the architectural treasures. In that case, we very often bring our interior noise with us which confines us to the obvious and blots out the "something heard beyond the stars".

Churches are best approached on foot, for this is holy ground, and although the conditions of contemporary London do not make it advisable for you to remove your shoes, nevertheless I am sure you are entirely right to escape from the confinement of vehicles to walk.

+Richard London:

Introduction

This book has been written because of a deep interest in, and abiding love of, the remaining City churches. It is not a detailed history of each church, but rather guidelines for the walker to identify the main points, and other interesting and even perhaps irrelevant details, which may well fire his imagination and enthusiasm to look more deeply elsewhere.

We have tried to show how all of the churches can be visited in sequence in a series of fascinating walks. When visiting a church, perhaps the best way to feel the atmosphere and see the church as a whole is to sit down for a while and look around you. After exploring the church it is always a good idea to walk around the outside, if this is possible, as you will often make other discoveries.

Many people will wonder and ask 'Why so many churches?'. To answer this it will be necessary to look back into the history of the City.

As the City developed and the population increased, the great religious foundations, with their wealth and royal connections, used some of their land to build churches to serve the ordinary citizens. City merchants and nobles also used their wealth to endow more churches, thus reflecting their importance. Older parish churches formed others, for instance St Mary Aldermary had four churches dedicated to St Mary formed from it. Every house was within the sound of church bells and, as the wealth of the City increased, so did the churches.

Those medieval churches were usually small and unimposing from the outside (St Ethelburga is an example of such a pre-Fire church, alas destroyed by an IRA bomb), but some religious houses were turned into parish churches, like St Bartholomew the Great and St Helen, and these buildings were naturally more substantial.

The City of London has always been a place of power, and of commerce. Merchants and noblemen had very considerable influence not only upon the citizens but also at the court of the King. It was to these merchants that the King looked when he needed money, and to the noblemen when the need was for an army. These 'City Fathers' also used their influence in the appointment of the clergy.

In days past the church was often used for reasons other than spiritual. Such things as plays and dances were held there, and stocks and pillories were frequently placed inside the churchyard. Archery practice was held there. The yew, still found today in many churchyards, supplied the best wood for bows. Water conduits and cisterns were often church property and were usually placed near the church so that the water could be blessed. Many churches had been granted the right of sanctuary; however a person in sanctuary was not permitted to be supplied with food, so the avenger and the hunted often came to terms. Churchwardens were responsible for all aspects of the vestry (parish) and also had the safe keeping of such things as maypoles, as well as the dress worn by the Morris Dancers.

Courts of Justice were often held in the church and contracts ratified by the altar. Foundling children were frequently named after the church where they were baptised. Another use of the medieval City church was that of a local bank. The strong chests can still be seen in some churches. They were not just used to keep the plate and registers but were also safes for the parish and parishioners' money. In times of danger churches also became warehouses for goods that might otherwise be stolen or destroyed. Samuel Pepys records how people filled the churches with their goods during the Great Fire of 1666.

The church tower was used as a lookout post, especially for the ever present fear of fires in the City, and parishes provided local people to fight fires. St Martin Outwich, alas no longer standing, was known as "St Martin with the Well and two Buckets".

Until the nineteenth century the towers of churches always stood well above the tops of all other buildings and must indeed have looked very graceful. They can be seen clearly in the illustration by Nicholas John Visscher. Today the City skyline is dominated by huge office blocks.

The City of London has withstood the tests of time, floods, invasions, battles and wars. However one devastating event transformed the churches and completely altered the mediaeval City. This was the Great Fire of September 2nd, 1666. It was possibly even more devastating than the Blitz of World War II.

The fire began in a baker's house in Pudding Lane and for some while did not cause undue alarm. There was nothing unusual about fires during this period. It must be remembered that most buildings were of wattle and daub with timber frames, standing cheek to jowl in the narrow streets. Their roofs were often thatched, and the upper floors overhanging and nearly touching the house opposite, so that they were easy prey for the sparks blown by the north-east wind early that morning. After a hot dry summer the houses burned like tinder. The warehouses along the banks of the Thames were full of unprotected inflammable materials, such as barrels of tallow, oil, bolts of cloth, and piles of timber and coal on the wharves added to the conflagration.

Although the Lord Mayor was called at this early stage he was unconcerned and uttered these scornful words: "Pish! A woman might pisse it out". Contemporary diarists, John Evelyn and Samuel Pepys, both recorded terrifying accounts of the three days that the fire raged unchecked.

There were a few primitive fire engines and leather fire buckets. People formed chains of fire-fighters using these buckets, but as the narrow streets were blocked with goods from the blazing houses it was impossible for them to be of much use. The Lord Mayor was urged to order the demolition of rows of houses in the path of the fire but, fearful of claims for compensation, he refused to do this. King Charles II and his brother, the Duke of York, played a leading role in fighting the fire and received great public acclaim for their actions. On Tuesday evening the King finally gave orders for gun powder to be used to blast houses not yet on fire, so as to create greater space and contain the fire. This, together with the dropping of the wind, combined to control the fire.

Almost four hundred acres of the City were destroyed. They included eighty seven churches and more than thirteen thousand houses. Nearly two hundred and fifty thousand people were homeless. On 13th September 1666 King Charles issued a proclamation that all new buildings must be constructed of stone or brick and the streets widened.

The churches suffered further losses not only in the Blitz during the Second World War, but also in the 19th century, when twenty churches were either destroyed or sold for commercial buildings. Most can now only be identified by a plaque.

One of the strangest happenings was to St Mary Aldermanbury, bombed in 1940. After the war the stones were sent to Westminster College, Fulton, Missouri, U.S.A. and re-erected as a memorial to Sir Winston Churchill. Today all that marks the site is a garden with a bust of William Shakespeare. Very often in the City a tiny garden, tucked away, is all that is left to remind us that there was once a church on the site.

St Paul's Cathedral, a magnificent building and Wren's masterpiece, situated near the centre of the City, has not been included in this book. The reason for this is that our book concerns only the parish churches.

There are two important necessities fundamental to these walks. One is food and the other toilets. Food and drink can be carried by the walker, but toilets pose more of a problem. There are several places where public toilets can be found, including the following railway and underground stations: Aldgate East, Bank, Blackfriars, Cannon Street, Liverpool Street and Mansion House. There are also two near St Paul's Cathedral and one outside the Guildhall Library.

The City is full of restaurants, pubs and sandwich bars, all open during the week, but nearly all closed on Saturdays, Sundays and public holidays. Also, from time to time, excellent refreshments can be obtained in some of the churches.

Opening times of the churches

Every effort has been made to ensure that the opening times of the churches are accurate. However sometimes information is not always readily available. In cases of difficulty we suggest telephoning the Archdeacon of London's office. Telephone number: 0207 488 2335.

Glory in St Vedast alias Foster

Medieval Religious Houses

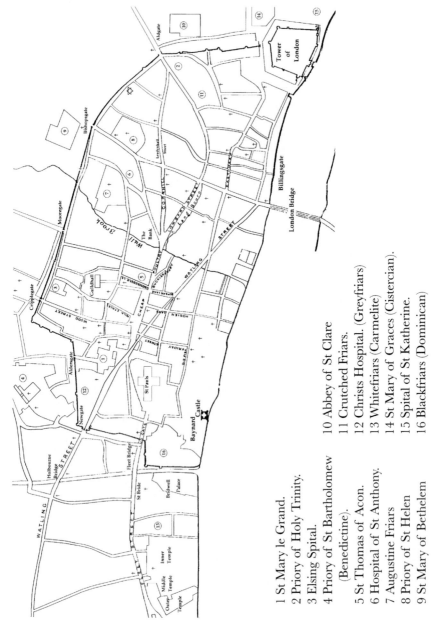

1 St Mary le Grand.
2 Priory of Holy Trinity.
3 Elsing Spital.
4 Priory of St Bartholomew (Benedictine).
5 St Thomas of Acon.
6 Hospital of St Anthony.
7 Augustine Friars
8 Priory of St Helen
9 St Mary of Bethelem

10 Abbey of St Clare
11 Crutched Friars.
12 Christs Hospital. (Greyfriars)
13 Whitefriars (Carmelite)
14 St Mary of Graces (Cistercian).
15 Spital of St Katherine.
16 Blackfriars (Dominican)

Walk 1
Aldgate to London Wall

St Botolph Aldgate, St Katherine Cree,
Spanish and Portuguese Synagogue,
St Andrew Undershaft,
St Helen, St Ethelburga,
St Botolph without Bishopsgate,
All Hallows London Wall.

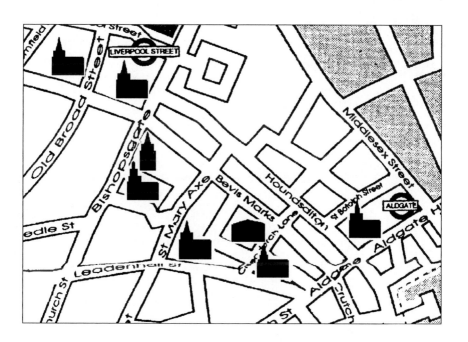

St Botolph Aldgate

Aldgate High Street, London EC1.
Open: Monday-Friday 10-3, Saturday closed,
Sunday 9-12.30.
Nearest Tube: Aldgate.

An ancient foundation. Given to the Priory of Holy Trinity
and Christchurch in 1125.
Rebuilt at the beginning of the 16th century.
Escaped the Great Fire.
Rebuilt in 1741 by George Dance the Elder.
Renovated in the 19th century by J F Bentley.

For over a thousand years a church has stood here, just outside
the gateway in the City wall. Nearby was an old moat called
Houndsditch, the name of which is still preserved in the
adjacent road.

St Botolph was at one time widely venerated throughout
England as the patron saint of travellers. Thus dedications to
him are found in churches at city gateways, quays and wharves
where trade and goods entered the city.

The area around the church was once part of the richest priory
in England before it was surrendered to Henry VIII (1509-
1547) at the Dissolution of the Monasteries in 1531. This
was the first and richest prize to fall into Henry's hands. St
Botolph Aldgate was rebuilt only a few years before the
Dissolution and escaped the Great Fire of 1666. However
due to much neglect it fell into a very bad state of repair and
was pulled down. It was rebuilt (1741-44) by George Dance
the Elder, who was also the architect of the Mansion House.

LOOK at the Rubens window
over the altar.

LOOK at the modern reredos
panels in batik by Thetis
Blacker (1982).

In the 19th century it was refurbished by J F Bentley, the
architect of Westminster Cathedral. Before Bentley started
his work, the church had almost nothing to recommend it,
and was empty and bare. He lowered the galleries and installed
light balustrades. The ceiling and the underside of the galleries
he enriched with fine plasterwork of angels and shields. He
also gave a great deal of attention to the windows, which are
of plain glass, allowing full daylight to enter.

Formerly one of the curiosities was the mummified head, supposedly of the Duke of Suffolk, Lady Jane Grey's father. He was beheaded in the Tower in 1554. This rather sensational object was for many years shown to visitors, but in 1968 was buried with other remains in the foundations of the new vestry.

Other famous people who have connections with this church include Daniel Defoe, the author of "Robinson Crusoe", who was married here in 1683, and the poet Edmund Spenser, who was born in the parish in 1552. Sir John Cass, who endowed the school which bears his name just along the road, was also born and baptised here. The tablet under the sword rest is dedicated to William Symington, an engineer who had built the first steamboat, the "Charlotte Dundas."

Thomas Bray was the rector here at the beginning of the 18th century. He was a very remarkable man and was instrumental in the establishment of both the Society for the Promotion of Christian Knowledge (S.P.C.K.) and the Society for the Propagation of the Gospel (S.P.G.) Today the church is the centre of Christian-Jewish understanding and in its crypt houses a centre for the homeless, which also undertakes to teach them a trade and re-house them.

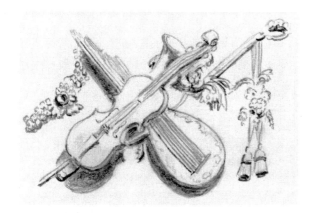

Trophy

LOOK at the organ built by Renatus Harris. The fine carving on the organ case is said to be the work of Grinling Gibbons. This was given by Thomas Whiting. It had been built for his house, but after the death of his wife, he gave it to St Botolph.

Nearest toilets: Liverpool Street Station.

To reach the next church, turn to your right as you leave St Botolph and cross the road at the lights. Keeping Sir John Cass school on your right, go across Mitre Street. At the junction of Fenchurch Street and Leadenhall Street notice the Aldgate Pump with the copper wolf's head. In the 15th century this was known as St Michael's Well. It was moved just a few feet in the 1860s, so that Fenchurch Street could be widened. In 1886 the well was filled in and the pump connected to the mains.

Now walk down Leadenhall Street and you arrive at St Katherine Cree.

St Katherine Cree

Leadenhall Street, London EC3.
Open: Monday-Friday 10-4.30, Saturday closed,
Sunday for services.
Nearest Tube: Aldgate.

Very ancient foundation.
First church built between 1280 and 1303.
Rebuilt in 1504 and again in 1630, perhaps by Inigo
Jones.
Suffered some damage during the Blitz.

The first reference to this church is in 1280 when it was
known as St Katherine de Christchurch at Alegate. It was
built on the land of the priory of Holy Trinity and was
known as Sanctae Katherinae Trinitatis Cree in 1308. Cree
is a corruption of Christ.

The church was rebuilt in 1504 and again in 1630, perhaps
by Inigo Jones: the first attempt at Renaissance or Classical
architecture in the City. The tower however is the original
one, built in 1504.

The doorway in Cree Lane is the one by which Bishop Laud
entered in January 1630 to consecrate the new church. The
choir sang , "Lift up your heads, O ye gates, and be ye lift
up, Ye everlasting doors, And the King of Glory shall come
in" (Psalm 24) . On entering the church Bishop Laud fell on
his knees and pronounced the place holy. Standing at the
Communion table, he took a book into his hand, putting
curses on all who should profane it by musters of soldiers,
keeping law courts or taking loads through it. He then gave
a blessing on all who should endow the church with plate or
ornaments. At each blessing he bowed to the east and
required the people to say "Amen!". In administering the
Sacrament he made many lowly bowings, walking back a
step or two and bowing again. Years later this episode was
to cost him his life, because during his trial his conduct on
this day was brought up and turned the case against him.
The Laud Chapel in the south-east corner of the church

was furnished by the Society of King Charles the Martyr.

The "Lion Sermon" preached every October 17, commemorates the deliverance of Sir John Gayer (Lord Mayor in 1646) from a lion whilst he was travelling in the Arabian desert. In gratitude he gave the whole proceeds of his journey to charity and determined that every year a sermon should be preached on the anniversary: a tradition which is continued to this day, thus demonstrating how this ancient church continues to serve the needs of the modern day.

A reminder of the earlier church is the Throckmorton Memorial. Sir Nicholas Throckmorton, who died in 1570, was Chief Butler of England under Queen Elizabeth I (1558-1603). His daughter married Sir Walter Raleigh. Throgmorton Street is named after him.

It is believed that Hans Holbein was buried in the earlier building. He had been staying with the Duke of Norfolk when he died of the plague.

A modern stained glass window and wooden wall plaque beneath commemorate the sinking of the troopship Lancastria and drowning of 5,000 people during the Second World War. The Survivors' Association had this erected, and a yearly service is held in June.

The garden that remains at the back of the church is part of the original garden of the priory, where in ancient days the monks used to tell their beads. In Elizabethan times plays were also acted here. In recent years part of this ground has been sold for office building, enabling much needed repairs of the church to be carried out.

LOOK for the font with Sir John Gayer's arms. The fleur de lys shows his royal descent.

LOOK at the cedarwood pulpit and its sounding board inlaid with seven varieties of wood. It was at one time used as a table in the vestry.

LOOK at the window over the altar.

LOOK at the organ built in 1685 by the famous Father Smith.

LOOK for the Lancastria window (and the wall plaque), commemorating the sinking of the troop ship, drowning 5,000 people.

The next stop is not a church, but a synagogue. Turn right into Creechurch Lane, walk to the end, then turn left and not very far along Bevis Marks is the synagogue.

Spanish & Portuguese Synagogue

A view of the synagogue through the gate

Look at the wooden oak benches brought from the older house of worship in Creechurch Lane.

ASK to see the painting of Moses and Aaron with the tablets of the Ten Commandments between them. It was at one time hung in the synagogue, but was removed as it was thought to contravene the Second Commandment.

The reach the next church, St Andrew Undershaft retrace your steps to St Katherine Cree. Turn right and walk down Leadenhall Street. The church stands on the junction of this street and Saint Mary Axe.

Bevis Marks, London EC3.
Open: Monday and Wednesday 11-1, Tuesday 10.30-4, Friday 11.30-1.
Sunday 11.30-1. Thursday and Saturday closed.
Nearest Tube: Aldgate.
Built in 1701.

The first Jewish house of worship in the City was established in 1657 in a house in Creechurch Lane, now marked by a plaque. This was founded by Jews from Spain and Portugal after the re-entry of Jews into England under Oliver Cromwell.

By the beginning of the 18th century the congregation had increased considerably, which required the building, in 1701, of the present synagogue in Bevis Marks, the oldest Jewish synagogue in the country. The name Bevis Marks is said by Stow to be a corruption of "Beuries Marks", since a large house and garden there were once the property of the Abbot of Bury. The synagogue remains unaltered today and still has all its original fittings. Practically no changes have occurred, except some reconstruction of the roof. The doorway of the west front has a key block inscribed AM 5461-1701.

The beautiful plain windows light a classically elegant and uncluttered interior, with the Ark built like a reredos at the east end. Oak benches were brought from Creechurch Lane Synagogue and are still to be found in the back rows of seats. Symbolism is found in many of the objects. The seven candelabra, still used to light the building, signify the seven days of the week; ten large brass candlesticks, six before the Ark and four on the Reading Desk, represent the Ten Commandments; and the twelve columns supporting the gallery are the twelve tribes of Israel.

Benjamin Disraeli's (or D'Israeli as his name was written) name is found in the Register of Births. He was Prime Minister of England in 1868 and again in 1874. His father quarrelled with the synagogue authorities and had all his children baptised as Christians. This enabled his son to become a Member of Parliament, as Jews were not permitted to do so until 1858.

St Andrew Undershaft

St Mary Axe, London EC3.
Not generally open to the public; contact St Helens.
Nearest Tube: Bank.

First mentioned in 1267.
Rebuilt in 1532.
Escaped the Fire of London.
Restored in 1875 and in 1930.

St Andrew Undershaft is known as Stow's church, and he referred to it as "the fair and beautiful parish church of Saint Andrew the Apostle". A new nave roof was installed in 1950, but retained the old bosses. The window in the west is of most beautiful 17th century glass, showing English Monarchs and heraldry. It was moved from the east by the Victorians. There is a great deal of 17th century carving in this church, of which the organ case is a fine example. There is also some 18th century ironwork. The font by Nicholas Stone pre-dates the Great Fire of 1666. Nicholas Stone was mason to James I (1603-1625) and Charles I (1625-1649). The following record was made by Stone on 13 November 1631. *"Agreed with Mr Jones, churchwarden of St Andrew Undershaft in the presence of Mr Godfrey and two others of that vestry to make for that church a font, the bowl to be of white marble 20 inches in diameter and to stand on a pillar of black marble fairly wrought and polished and set up for the sum of £16. The work to be done as soon as may be".* The carved font cover is in harmony with the pulpit, as it is said to have been done by Grinling Gibbons.

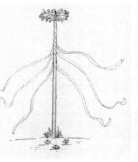

Stow in poverty was given a licence to beg by James I. He died in 1605 and is buried here. The alabaster monument dedicated to him is in the north-east corner, and he is shown sitting at a desk writing. Every year a new quill is put into his hand, when a memorial service is held.

There is a modern brass tablet to Hans Holbein the Younger, who was living in the parish just before his death in 1543.

Maypole

The name "Undershaft" refers to a maypole, taller than the church tower. It played the central part in the festival of returning spring. There is no record of when the first pole was erected but

LOOK at the fine monument to John Stow.

LOOK. at the sanctuary knocker on the main door.

WHY is William III in the window instead of Charles II?

the following story of the last time the maypole was erected is of interest. The day came to be known as Evil Day because on 1st May 1517 a serious riot broke out in the middle of the festivities. A cry was raised that there were too many foreigners dumping their goods and taking away the Londoners' trade. A group of apprentices began to plunder the homes of any foreigners that they could find and a free fight took place on the streets. Swift punishment followed and 14 of the instigators were hanged in convenient spots about the City.

The church is not generally open to the public. It has been renovated to accommodate church meetings and Sunday Schools and is now connected with St Helen, the next church on this walk.

Detail of carving on the organ

John Stow's memorial

To reach the next church, St Helen, cross the road and walk to the right, taking the next turning on your left, Great St Helen's, and you will see the church on the right.

8

St Helen

Bishopsgate, Great St Helen's, London EC3.
Open: Monday-Friday 9-5, Tuesday 9-12,
Saturday closed, Sunday services 10am and 7pm.
Nearest Tube: Liverpool Street.

Ancient foundation. Built in 1326.
Survived the Great Fire.
Rebuilt in 1682 by Sir Christopher Wren.

Combined parish with St Martin Outwitch (destroyed in 1796 and finally sold in 1874), and houses many of its monuments.

Little more than a decade ago St Helen was well hidden from passers by. New buildings have unkindly exposed her hiding place of centuries. The exterior walls present a wonderful patchwork of history, showing many secret half windows now blocked. A new vicarage was built at the south side in 1964.

LOOK at the Shakespeare window

LOOK for the tomb of John & Alice Spencer with an hour glass on the top.

The church is entered by a carved doorway (there are two others on the right hand side a quarter of the way down). Descend some steps into a spacious and well used church. The main feature is the double aisle, as this was originally two buildings which were combined at the Dissolution of the Monasteries to form one church. On the north side in ancient times was a Benedictine Nunnery; the parish church was built next to it. At the Dissolution the partition between the convent and the parish church was removed, forming the building we see today.

LOOK at the bell tower built on the inside by Wren.

In mediaeval times the church was famed for possessing a portion of the True Cross.

The north wall is full of history; passing the Shakespeare window and following the wall you will find an old arch, now blocked, which was once the main entrance from the convent. There are the remains of the stairs from which the nuns passed from their dormitory to their devotions, and a rare 15th century hagioscope (squint) survives, from which vantage point the nuns could see the altar without entering the church. They may have been pious but they were also human: in 1365 they were officially reproved

The famous 15th century "squint", through which nuns used to listen to services.

"for kissing secular people - and wearing ostentatious veils", and the Prioress was restricted to keeping only two dogs!

One of the most interesting memorials is to Francis Bancroft in 1727. He was an eccentric man who amassed a vast fortune by doubtful means. He erected his tomb and explained the reasons in the following inscription. *"The ground whereon this tomb stands was purchased of the Parish in MDCCXXIII by Francis Bancroft Esq., for the interment of himself and friends only (and was confirmed to him by the Dean and Chapter of St Paul's) and in his life time he erected this tomb and settled part of his estate in London and Middlesex for the beautifying and keeping the same in good repair".*

The tomb was of a square shape and covered with a hinged lid so that it could be opened for viewing the corpse, which was embalmed according to the deceased's wishes. A solemn inspection of the body took place periodically by the officers of the Company of Drapers until the end of the 19th century, by which time this was not too pleasing a task as the art of the embalmer had proved inadequate. The original monument was placed beneath the floor in the 19th century.

Sir Thomas Gresham was buried here. For many years there was a bracket with his helmet, which tradition said was carried before the corpse at his funeral in 1579.

William & Alice Markeby

Nearest toilets: Liverpool Street Station.

It is only a short walk to St Ethelburga the Virgin. Walk straight ahead and turn right into Bishopsgate, past St Helen's Place and after a few more steps you will find the church.

You can see how St Helen was once two churches

St Ethelburga the Virgin

Bishopsgate, London EC2.
Nearest Tube: Liverpool Street.
Open occasionally, apply to the church.

Ancient Saxon foundation.
First mentioned in 1250.
Rebuilt in the 15th century.
Repaired in 1612 and a small steeple added in 1620.
Extensive alterations by Sir Ninian Comper in 1912.
Destroyed by terrorists' bombs in 1993.
Rebuilt by Purcell Miller Tritton in November 2002.

St Ethelburga is believed to be the only Anglican church in this country dedicated to this saint, who was the daughter of Annas, King of the East Anglians. Her brother Erconwald became Bishop of London in 675 and founded the great Abbey at Barking, over which he placed his sister as abbess.

Many writers have remarked how easy it is to pass the church by, as it looks so small. Until 1932 the church was completely obscured by two picturesque but ramshackle shops built by the churchwardens in 1570 to augment its income. Attached to the front of the church, they consisted of two rooms with sleeping quarters over the porch, making the entrance a dusky tunnel. Due to sensitive restoration and renovation by Sir Ninian Comper, the church retained the original feeling of churches before the Great Fire.

Sadly St Ethelburga was destroyed by terrorists bombs in 1993. As there was little fire many shattered fragments remained which have been used in the rebuilding. It was reconsecrated in November 2002 and is now a centre for peace and reconciliation.

There was a window commemorating the voyages of Henry Hudson and his companions. On 19th April 1607 they took communion here before starting their voyage to discover a passage via the North Pole to China & Japan. The chalice used is one of the treasures today.

At one time there was a pathway from the garden leading to St Helen's Place, site of a nunnery.

The font cover came from St Swithin London Stone. The unusual crown surmounting the cover is a Jacobite symbol for "The King over the water". Around the bowl, in brass letters, was one of the longest palindromes, inscribed in Greek: "Nipson anomeema mee monan opsin"meaning (Cleanse my sin not only my face). This is also to be found around the font at St Martin Ludgate (Walk 6).

The Jacobean font and cover

St Ethelburga from a photograph taken in 1906

Painting by Terence Dalley before the bombs in 1993

To reach the next church, turn right as you leave, and walk down the street to the lights, at the junction with Camomile & Wormwood Streets. Turn left and cross at the lights, then cross Wormwood Street. Just past the shops on your left is St Botolph.

13

St Botolph without Bishopsgate

Bishopsgate, London EC2.
Open: Monday-Friday 8-5.30.
Nearest Tube: Liverpool Street.

Very ancient foundation.
First mentioned in 1274.
The earliest church restored many times .
Taken down and rebuilt in 1725 by James Gold.

Bishopsgate parish church is situated at the junction of Houndsditch with Bishopsgate and surrounded by a pleasant churchyard, which in 1863 was the first to be turned into a public garden, arousing widespread indignation at the time. Nearby are reproductions of two mitres, episcopal symbols, marking the site of the Roman gate of the City and reminding us of the two bishops who were responsible for maintaining it, St Erconwald and Bishop William.

The church is built on an extremely old hallowed site where, it is believed, there were 7th and 8th century Saxon altars. The earliest church dates from the beginning of the 13th century and was restored many times, once at the personal expense of the Lord Mayor, Sir William Allen, in 1571-72. This building lasted until 1725 when it was taken down and rebuilt by James Gold. After the Second World War, Cachemaille-Day thoroughly restored and redecorated it, making alterations in the Sanctuary. Around the nave are recorded on separate tablets the names of all the rectors from the 14th century onwards.

ON ENTERING THE CHURCH DOOR LOOK for the two stained glass windows depicting the Last Supper, and note the spilt salt (bad luck).

LOOK for the font, lectern and sword rest, and the Royal Artillery Chapel.

Among the famous who have connections with this church are Sir Paul Pindar, Ambassador to Turkey in 1611, who is buried here, and Edward Alleyn 1566-1626, celebrated Elizabethan actor-manager, founder of Dulwich College, who was baptised here, as was the poet John Keats. The font is still in use today.

One of the most unusual monuments was a grave for a Persian merchant buried in the churchyard on 10 August 1626, inscribed in both English and Persian. Sadly, due to renovations in the churchyard, this unusual tombstone is no longer visible.

The red brick parish hall behind the church is now used by the Worshipful Company of Fan Makers but formerly was one of the City's Charity Schools, as the two charming statues of 18th century children set in niches testify.

The old priory of Bethlehem, commonly known as "Bedlam," stood next to the church for over 300 years. At the Dissolution of the Monasteries in 1535 Henry VIII gave this priory to the citizens of London as a hospital for lunatics. Thus the corruption of the name passed into the English language.

Outside the church, on the way to All Hallows, LOOK for the Parish Hall, once the school house, and notice the figures of 18th century children.

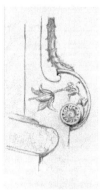

Decoration on the corner of the pulpit.

Turkish Kiosk

To reach the last church on this walk, turn right as you leave the front door and then right again down the pathway. On the right hand side behind the back of the church is the Parish Hall, and a little further on is the Turkish Bath, now a restaurant. Continue on into Old Broad Street, turn left, and at the traffic lights turn right into London Wall. After a short distance you arrive at All Hallows. Enter by the side door. You will have to ring the bell.

15

All Hallows London Wall

London Wall, London EC2.
Open: Friday 11-3.
Nearest tube: Liverpool Street.

First mentioned in 1120.
Escaped the Great Fire, but fell into a terrible state of disrepair.
Rebuilt by George Dance the Younger, 1765-67.
Severely damaged in Word War II.
Rebuilt in 1960-2.

From the outside All Hallows gives the impression of being a House of Correction rather than a City Church. It must possess the least attractive exterior of all the churches, with its plain walls unbroken by windows or ornamentation. That is because this church was originally built on the old City wall, and, like St Mary Woolnoth (see Walk 2), this side was never intended to be exposed to the public gaze.

It is now a Guild Church, and the home of the London and South East Team of Christian Aid. On entering the church, if you look carefully at the pulpit you will see that, in order to enter it, you must go into the vestry (built on one of the bastions of the Roman Wall) which is <u>outside</u> the wall, and so outside the City! The hour glass beside the pulpit, although modern, strikes a cautious note.

The church was completely rebuilt in 1756-67 by George Dance the younger. The very elegant style, with its perfect proportions, is crowned by the white and gold of the plaster ceiling. The painting over the altar "Ananias restoring the sight to St Paul" is by Dance's brother, Nathaniel Dance-Holland.

Surviving many vicissitudes and periods of neglect, it was severely damaged in World War II and left as a ruin for 20 years. In 1960 it was restored by David Nye and given a new lease of life as the headquarters of the Council for the Care of Churches.

In mediaeval times All Hallows was noted for the many hermits or anchorites who lived in cells built onto the wall, near the church. They lived there by choice, completely walled in, and received alms and food from the local inhabitants. Some of the hermits even boasted servants! The most famous of these was known as "Simon the Anker". He wrote a book called "The Fruyts of Redempcyon", printed by Wynkyn de Worde in 1514.

LOOK at the pulpit, with its entrance outside the City.

The church has had many literary rectors; one, S J Stone, wrote the well known hymn "The Church's One Foundation".

LOOK at the picture over the altar.

Before the 1939-45 war this church was a refuge for girls coming every day to work in the City. Arriving very early on the cheap workmen's trains, they would then have an hour or so to wait before their offices opened. All Hallows on the Wall opened every morning from 7-9 especially for these office girls. As many as three hundred came every day to keep warm and dry.

A close view of the top of the font

Walk 2
Cornhill to Walbrook

St Peter upon Cornhill,   St Michael Cornhill,
St Edmund King and Martyr,   St Clement,
St Mary Abchurch.
St Mary Woolnoth of the Nativity,
St Stephen Walbrook.

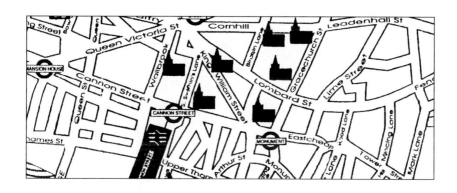

St Peter upon Cornhill

London EC3.
Closed, but apply to St Helen.
Nearest Tube: Bank.

Ancient foundation, AD 791.
Restored in the reign of Edward IV (1461-1483).
Destroyed by the Great Fire.
Rebuilt by Sir Christopher Wren in 1681.

St Peter's tower stands out upon Cornhill as a landmark for all to see. It boasts the oldest foundation of any of the City Churches. A tablet in the church claims its foundation by King Lucius in AD 791. It was this very ancient foundation that prompted a squabble in 1471, during the ecclesiastical processions through the City at Whitsuntide. The parishioners of St Peter, St Magnus and St Nicholas Cole fought amongst themselves as to which of their rectors should take precedence in the celebrations. This dispute continued for many years until finally the Lord Mayor and Aldermen decided upon St Peter on the grounds of its ancient foundation.

Because of its age and the precedence given to its rector it was specifically excluded from the Union of Benefices Act of 1871, which led to the demolition of many parish churches. Another proof of its importance is the fact that the church supported a grammar school, which was found only in churches with cathedral status. Stow records in his Survey of London (1603) that there was a *"table wherein is written that Lucius founded the church to be an Archbishops See and Metropolitan or chief church of his kingdom and that it so endured for 400 years until the arrival of Augustine"*

The font was presented by Samuel Purchas in 1682, but the very finely carved cover is a reminder of the earlier church, as it is the only portion of church furniture saved from the Great Fire.

Near the screen is a particularly poignant memorial, crowned with seven cherubs' heads. This records the deaths of seven small Woodmason children, whose parents went out one evening to a ball for the Queen's birthday at St James's Palace. On returning they found their home burnt and all their seven children dead, together with other members of the household. More people died in this fire than perished during the Great Fire.

LOOK at the Woodmasons monument.

By the entrance, fixed to a wall, are some fine examples of 17th century bread shelves, which were once filled with loaves at the harvest festival, afterwards distributed to the children and poor.

The organ was built by Father Schmidt, although it has been much restored. The original keyboard, which was used by Mendelssohn several times, can still be seen in the vestry.

The Poulters' Company hold their annual service here on 8th February.

St Peter is now a Guild Church and connected with St Helen. Sunday Schools are held here.

Pew End

St Peter upon Cornhill, hidden from Cornhill.

Nearest toilets:Bank Underground Station

To reach the next church, St Michael Cornhill, go back into Cornhill and turn left. A little way along is the church, just set back.

21

St Michael Cornhill

Cornhill, London EC3.
Open: Monday-Friday 8-5.30, Sunday Service 11 (not
August).
Nearest Tube: Bank.

Founded in Saxon Times.
First mentioned 1055.
Destroyed by the Great Fire.
Rebuilt by Sir Christopher Wren in 1672.
Tower rebuilt in 1721 by Nicholas Hawksmoor.
Restored in 1860 by Sir Gilbert Scott

The foundations of this church are built upon the site of the
Roman Forum, centre of all activity of ancient London, so that
it is not surprising that its origins are lost in antiquity, and the
first mention is found in the Evesham Chronicle. This states that
in 1055 a priest named Alnothus gave the living of St Michael's
as a gift to the Abbot and Convent of Evesham.

The name signifies its dedication to St Michael and All Angels,
and Cornhill its situation. The beautiful pinnacled tower, an
imitation of Magdalen College, Oxford was Wren's last piece of
architectural work. The church was virtually destroyed in the
Great Fire, except for its tower, which housed the famous peal of
12 bells. It was, however, rebuilt by Wren. Fifty years later, as an
old man of 90, he made the design for the tower, which was
completed by Hawksmoor.

Sir Gilbert Scott was responsible in 1858-60 for the porch facing
Cornhill with its imposing representation of St Michael and the
devils; and for the many alterations inside the church, which have
caused much controversy but at the time were praised by Prince
Albert, Consort of Queen Victoria.

A beautiful carving of a pelican feeding its young, an old symbol
of the church, is found under the west window. This was formerly
over the altar, but during Sir Gilbert Scott's restorations was taken
down and would have been sold for scrap but for the rector's
daughter, who gave a workman half a crown (12½p) to stop him
taking it away.

The pew ends, carved with plants and herbs of the bible, are by W Gibbs Rogers, a noted Victorian woodcarver.

As you turn into the alley at the side of the church you will find all that remains of the churchyard. On the south side you pass the site of the first coffee house in England! Set up in 1657 by the servant of a Turkey merchant, one Pasqua Rosee, and his friend, who also sold coffee in a tent in the churchyard.

LOOK for the carving of the pelican feeding its young.

LOOK at the carved pew ends.

The pelican feeding its young

The route to the next church, which is behind St Michael, is only a short walk. Go down St Michael's Alley at the side of the church, go across Castle Court and into George Yard, and on your right you will see the side and back of St Edmund. On reaching Lombard Street, turn right and there you are.

23

St Edmund King and Martyr

Lombard Street, London EC3.
Open: Monday-Friday 8.30-5.00; Sunday for services by
"Deeper Light", from West Africa.
Nearest Tube: Bank.

Saxon origins.
Damaged in the Great Fire.
Rebuilt by Sir Christopher Wren in 1690.

This church was originally known as St Edmund Grasschurch
because of its proximity to the herb market nearby.

The earliest reference to this church is of its being given by Queen
Matilda, wife of Henry I (1100-1135), to the prior of Holy Trinity
in 1108. This is the only church to be dedicated to the Saint who
was the King of East Anglia. He was taken prisoner by the Danes
and shot to death with arrows. In 870 his followers built the large
abbey of Bury St Edmund's over his remains.

The church was destroyed by the Great Fire and then rebuilt by
Sir Christopher Wren, but completed, it is believed, by his
surveyor, Robert Hooke, in 1690. It was amalgamated with the
parish of St Nicholas Acon, which was destroyed at the same
time but not rebuilt. Later still the parishes of St Dionis
Backchurch (demolished in 1878) and All Hallows Lombard
Street (demolished in 1938) were joined with St Edmund. The
tower of All Hallows was taken to Twickenham and joined to
the newly built church, where it can be seen clearly from the
A30.

The lectern

The individual steeple was added by Wren in 1706 and, together
with the projecting clock, makes an attractive addition to Lombard
Street. The interior, with its dark panelling, carved ornamental
urns on the choir stalls and richly stained glass windows, gives
the effect of a private chapel.

The stained glass was originally intended for St Paul's and was
made in Munich. However, objections were made to angels
clothed in red instead of white! It then lay for many years in the
crypt of St Paul's, eventually finding its way to St Edmund as a

memorial to the Duke of Clarence, eldest son of King Edward LOOK at the altar table. VII (1901-1910) who died in 1892. This and the window of St Andrew Undershaft (Walk 1) are two of the finest examples of 17th century glass in the City. The altar is a very fine Jacobean table. On the ceiling of the semi-circular dome is a painting from earlier times.

LOOK up at the steeple when you leave.

There are three royal hatchments on the east wall, those of Princess Charlotte, who died in childbirth in 1817, Edward Duke of Kent (father of Queen Victoria), who died in 1820, and King George IV, who died in 1830. Restoration was carried out in 1864-1880, when the demand for space seems to have been as great as it is today, as part of the small frontage on one side of the entrance was let for a gunsmith's shop and the other side for a shed to house the parish fire engine.

In 1716 Joseph Addison (1672-1719) married the Dowager Countess of Warwick and Holland here, an act they both lived to regret.

In the 1914-18 war it was one of the few churches to be hit by a bomb and fragments are still kept in the vestry. It was also damaged during World War II by incendiaries, and the coat of arms of Queen Anne (1665-1714) was destroyed. Modern restoration was carried out by Rodney Tatchell.

Lantern

Old fire engine

The route to the next church is very simple. Cross Lombard Street and into St Clement's Lane opposite. At the far end on the left is the church.

25

Oranges and Lemons

Bull's eyes and targets
Say the bells of St Margaret's
Brickbats and tiles
Say the bells of St Giles'
Oranges and lemons
Say the bells of St Clement's
Pancake and fritters
Say the bells of St Peter's
Two sticks and an apple
Say the bells at Whitechapel
Old father Baldpate
Say the bells at Aldgate
Pokers and tongs
Say the bells of St John's
Kettles and pans
Say the bells of St Anne's
You owe me five farthings
Say the bells of St Martin's
When will you pay me
Say the bells at Old Bailey
When I grow rich
Say the bells of Fleet Ditch
Pray when will that be
Say the bells at Stepney
I'm sure I don't know
Says the bells at Bow
Here comes a candle to light you to bed
Here comes a chopper to chop off your head.

St Clement

Eastcheap, St Clement's Lane, London EC3.
Open: Monday-Friday 9-5.
Nearest Tube: Monument.

Tenth Century. First recorded priest 1309.
Destroyed in the Great Fire.
Rebuilt by Sir Christopher Wren in 1683-7.
Restored and rearranged in 1872 by William Butterfield.

The dedication is to St Clement, who was the third Bishop of Rome after St Peter. He fell victim to Roman persecution and in AD 100 was cast into the sea with an anchor around his neck. He became the patron saint of sailors.

The church is now situated in a lane, but used to be in the main thoroughfare until the widening of King William Street left it hidden in the alley. Its ancient foundation is confirmed by its name appearing in a charter dated 1067 confirming grants of livings by William the Conqueror to Westminster Abbey. In the fourteenth century the name appears as St Clement Candlewickstrate, which was the old name for Cannon Street.

It was one of the first churches to be burnt in the Great Fire, which started very close by in Pudding Lane. It was completely rebuilt by Sir Christopher Wren in 1683-7, and was united with the parish of St Martin Orgar. (Orgamus, a Dane, had presented the living to St Paul's in 900. The church was destroyed in the Great Fire and never rebuilt).

Surviving an order for its demolition in 1834, St Clement succumbed to restoration and rearrangements in 1872 by William Butterfield. Thus its unpretentious exterior gives no hint of the extraordinary oblong interior with its dark wood panels, with turquoise and gold paint on the pillars and walls. The ceiling, which is unusually lofty, is also painted dark turquoise but enlivened with a huge wreath of gilded fruit and flowers, almost identical with those at St Mary Abchurch. The clear glass windows show off one of the most beautiful pulpits of the City churches, with its sounding box dancing with carved cherubs blowing horns. Sir Ninian Comper painted the altar piece a startling blue and gold.

ASK to see the font cover.

The organ is by Renatus Harris, and Edward Purcell, son of the composer Henry, was organist here for some time.

LOOK at the sounding box over the pulpit..

William Gladstone, Queen Victoria's Prime Minister, liked the the 17th century font so much that he used to bring his small grandchildren to see it.

ASK to see the bread shelves.

This church vies with St Clement Danes, in the Aldwych, to be the St Clement of the nursery rhyme. Spanish oranges used to be unloaded at a nearby quay, perhaps giving strength to its claim. St Clement is one of the smallest parish churches in the City. It has a sad and neglected feeling.

Bread Shelves

To walk to St Mary Abchurch turn left and at the junction with King William Street turn left again. At the traffic lights turn right into Cannon Street; now take the second on the right into Abchurch Lane.

28

St Mary Abchurch

Abchurch Lane, London EC4.
Open: Apply to the Church Secretary, 1 Abchurch Yard.
Nearest Tube: Monument.

First mentioned in the 12th century.
Destroyed in the Great Fire.
Rebuilt by Sir Christopher Wren in 1686.
Damaged during the Blitz in the Second World War, and
restored by Godfrey Allen.

St Mary Abchurch stands in Abchurch Yard, originally the burial
ground of the church, its boundaries now marked by posts. The
name Abchurch may refer to a now forgotten benefactor called
Abba or perhaps to Upchurch, as the name is spelt in early
documents. The gift of the living was granted to the Master of
Corpus Christi College, Cambridge in 1568, where it still remains.

The courtyard is tiled with circles of brick and wedges of slate
and stone set inside, like a cake, with tubs of flowers in the centre.
On the notice board attached to the church is a badge of the
Worshipful Company of Gardeners.

Cluster of
cherubs

St Mary was completely burnt in the Great Fire, and the
rebuilding by Sir Christopher Wren took five years. It was
completed in 1686 at a cost of £5,000. Wren, who was
experimenting with domes at that time, designed one for the
church that is considered an architectural tour de force. The
painting was not added until 1708 and was the work of a
parishioner, William Snow. The church is almost square and
measures 63ft x 60ft, with a spire of 140ft. It is the least altered
of Wren's churches.

Outstanding examples of Grinling Gibbons' carving are to be
seen in the altar piece, with its gilded pelican symbolising sacrifice,
charity and piety. This is the largest and only authenticated work
of his in the City churches. His receipts are among parish records
now preserved in the Guildhall Library. The pelican over the
door was once the original weather vane, which became unsafe
and was replaced in 1764. After the beauty of the sounding

Dog in kennel

board at St Clement you would hardly expect to find that the very next church would have one to equal it... but it does! The original boxed pews can still be found on three sides of the church. Underneath the pews on the south side there used to be cupboards or kennels. These were for the use of dog-owning parishioners, enabling them to bring their dogs to church, a unique service!

LOOK at the pelicans.

LOOK at the font.

LOOK at the pulpit and sounding box.

ASK to see the beadle's goldheaded stick.

BE SURE to look at the dome.

The west gallery was once reserved for the boys of Merchant Taylors' School, which stood in Suffolk Lane until 1875.

The organ is new, replacing one damaged in the blitz. It is built into a carved oak case dated 1717, brought from All Hallows Bread Street, which was demolished in 1877.

The Victorian glass and tiled floor were destroyed during the Second World War, but were restored by Walter Hughes. It was during a bombing raid that a flagstone was dislodged in the churchyard to reveal long forgotten vaults. One was dated 1690 and the other was 14th century. It was once proposed to convert them into a crypt chapel but lack of funds prevented this.

St Mary Abchurch is now a Guild Church.

The walk to the next church takes 2-3 minutes. When you leave this church turn right, follow the passageway, Sherborne Lane, back into King William Street and turn left. You will then see St Mary Woolnoth on your right about 100 yards away.

Glory in St Vedast Foster

St Mary Woolnoth of the Nativity

Lombard Street, London EC3.
Open: Monday to Friday 7.30-5.
Nearest Tube: Bank.

First Mentioned in 1191.Rebuilt in 1438. Damaged in the
Great Fire. Repaired by Sir Christopher Wren.
Rebuilt in 1716-27 by Nicholas Hawksmoor.

The first record of the church was in 1191. It was called
Wilnotmaricherche. The name comes from a rare dedication to
the Virgin Mary (in full St Mary Woolnoth of the Nativity). The
woolstaple was a place for weighing wool and stood in the nearby
churchyard of St Mary Woolchurch Haw, destroyed in the Great
Fire and now united with this church. Noth is a corruption of
Neath meaning near. At this time wool was brought up the Wall
Brook in barges and unloaded into the churchyard. This is a good
example of how the church and trade guilds worked closely
together. Another possible explanation for Woolnoth is that a
benefactor in 1133 was called Wulnoth de Walebrok and his name
may have been adopted in gratitude.

Whilst excavating the foundations of the present church, traces
of a timber Saxon structure were discovered. Evidence of two
earlier religious buildings were revealed, both pagan: one for
nature worship, the other a Roman temple.

In the early 18th century, the condition of the church became
dangerous. The parishioners petitioned parliament for a grant
to build a new church. Money came from a fund which was started
originally for rebuilding the City after the Great Fire. St Mary
Woolnoth was demolished, and in 1716 rebuilt by Nicholas
Hawksmoor. This was his only City church.

Considered by many writers the most original church exterior in
the City, the total difference between the north and south
elevations is due to the fact that before the construction of King
William Street only one side would ever be seen; it was not
expected that this other part of the church would eventually be
revealed.

The church interior is not imposing. The ceiling is covered in blue and gold stars and the ubiquitous cherubs' heads are placed all around. An imposing chandelier hangs in the church, a memorial to a former churchwarden, Colonel Buxton.

The tomb of Sir Martin Bowes, a Goldsmith and Lord Mayor 1545-6, was under the altar, and his instructions were that his banners should be hung there. This tomb was destroyed in the Great Fire, but the banners have been renewed from time to time by the Goldsmiths' Company. His helmet, gauntlet and spurs are preserved in a glass case. At his death in 1546 he left a cross of gold set with pearls and precious stones to hang at the collar of gold, which the Lord Mayor continues to wear at high feasts. He also left to the Goldsmiths' Company a sum of money to pay for an annual sermon on St Martin's Day. The Company were to attend and enjoy a dinner afterwards. This event ceased some years ago during the time that the church was closed for the building of the Bank Station.

Edward Lloyd, the founder of Lloyd's, was buried in St Mary's in 1712. In 1931 the tablet to his memory was placed in the church.

LOOK at the tablet on the wall to Edward Lloyd.

Simon Eyre the founder of Leadenhall was also buried here in 1445.

The site of the crypt beneath the church was sold in 1900, for conversion to the underground station's booking hall.

The church was in the patronage of the prioress of St Helen Bishopsgate until the Dissolution. In 1952 it was created a Guild Church, which means that it is no longer encumbered with parish duties, and can pursue a specialised ministry of its own choosing. A healing ministry has been founded to help those suffering from stress and tension, and there is a great feeling of peace in the church.

St Mary has been threatened with destruction on a number of occasions in 1863, 1897, 1900, 1920 and 1926, but it still stands proudly over the station.

The ubiquitous cherubs

There is now a short walk to the last church. At the lights cross over King William Street, now turn to your right and follow the road round past the Mansion House (the home of the Lord Mayor), then turn left into Walbrook, and ahead of you is St Stephen.

St Mary Woolnoth of the Nativity

St Stephen Walbrook

Walbrook, London EC4.
Open: Monday-Thursday 9-5, Friday 9-3.
Nearest Tube: Bank

First mentioned in 1096, when it was on the west bank of the brook.
Given to Colchester Abbey.
Rebuilt on the east bank in 1430.
Destroyed in the Great Fire.
Rebuilt by Sir Christopher Wren.
Damaged during Second World War.

Eudo, Dapifer (steward) to William the Conqueror (1066-1087), and Governor of Colchester, made a gift of St Stephen to his Abbey at Colchester in 1096. The first building was erected on the west bank of the Wall Brook, once a turbulent stream, now hidden under the road; but it was rebuilt on the east bank in 1430. The church was completely burnt in the Great Fire, except for its steeple and bells, which were not melted. It was rebuilt by Sir Christopher Wren, but on a smaller scale. Sir Christopher lived for a few years at No 5 Walbrook and worshipped here. St Stephen is considered to be one of his masterpieces, the dome being a rehearsal for that of St Paul's and the first to be built in England. The steeple was not added until 1717. The spire is 130ft high.

Bomb damage in the Second World War was repaired by Godfrey Allen, but by 1982 the structure had become dangerous and the church closed. It has recently been restored through the generous support of the public and in particular Lord Palumbo, who is one of the Churchwardens.

The inside of the church, with its beautiful decorations of white marble rosettes, glistens and gleams like the icing of a huge cake. The magnificent round altar by Henry Moore was presented by Lord Palumbo and placed under the centre of the dome. Weighing ten tons, it looks like an enormous white cheese but blends well in the middle of the church, with attractive pews placed in a circle around the altar.

The monument on the north side is to the playwright and architect Sir John Vanburgh, who built Blenheim Palace and Harewood House. He died in 1726. His witty epitaph, "Lie heavy on him earth-he laid many heavy loads on thee", was attributed to his contemporary Nicholas Hawksmoor. The painting of "The stoning of St Stephen" is by Benjamin West, the only American to become President of the Royal Academy.

William le Clerk met his death in the belfry in 1728, where he had climbed to search for pigeons' eggs. He fell on to one of the beams and "the whole of his body was ruptured and crushed".

In 1953 The Samaritans were founded in the crypt by the Rector, Prebendary Dr Chad Varah, who is still the Rector.

DO WALK round and look at the Henry Moore altar.

SEE the memorial to Sir John Vanburgh.

SIT down and look all around, feeling the peace and tranquillity.

The font

The altar

Walk 3
Tower Hill to Garlick Hill

All Hallows by the Tower, St Olave Hart Street,
All Hallows Staining and St Katherin Coleman,
St Margaret Pattens, St Dunstan in the East,
St Mary at Hill, St Magnus the Martyr,
St Martin Orgar,
St Michael Paternoster Royal,
St James Garlickhythe.

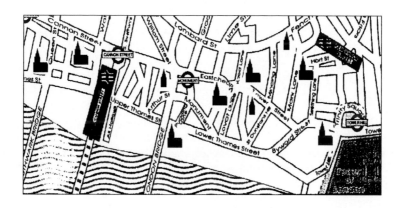

All Hallows by the Tower

Also known as All Hallows Barking.
Great Tower Street, London EC3.
Open: Monday-Friday 10-6, Saturday afternoon, Sunday.
Nearest Tube: Tower Hill.

First Saxon church built 6th-7th century, burnt down in 1087.
Fourteenth century crypt.
Narrowly escaped the Great Fire. Samuel Pepys watched the
progress of the fire from the church tower.
The church was entirely gutted in the Blitz. Rebuilt in 1957.

All Hallows Barking recalls its long connection with Barking
Abbey in Essex. It also has a long association with the Crown,
who were great benefactors. Richard I (1189-99) founded a lady
chapel on the north side and it was said that his 'lion heart' was
buried under the high altar. Edward I (1272-1307) donated a
picture of the Virgin Mary, and the Pope granted an indulgence
to all pilgrims worshipping there. Later Edward IV (1461-83)
gave licence to his cousin John, Earl of Worcester to found a
brotherhood there. Richard III (1483-85) rebuilt the chapel, and
a dean and six priests were added.

With its nearness to the Tower of London, it is indeed rich in
history. Many of those executed on Tower Hill were buried here.
The body of Archbishop Laud (1573-1645) was here for some
eighteen years, before being transferred to Oxford.

Lancelot Andrewes (1555-1626), who was in succession Bishop
of Chichester, Ely and Winchester, was baptised here, and he
always had a great affection for All Hallows. William Penn (1644-
1718), the founder of Pennsylvania, who was born on Tower
Hill, was also baptised here. He obtained a grant of land in
America, in settlement of a debt owed by the King to his father.
There is another American connection: John Quincy Adams
(1767-1848), sixth President, was married here in 1797.

The church was saved during the Great Fire largely by the efforts
of Samuel Pepys and Admiral Sir William Penn, the father of
William of Pennsylvania. As the flames were at the door (until the

Blitz the scorch marks could still be seen) they organised the putting out of the fire before it could get a hold.

Pepys recorded it in his famous diary.

About two in the morning my wife calls me up and tells me of the new cryes of fire, it being come to Barking Church, which is at the bottom of our lane. But going to the fire I find that by the blowing of houses, and the great help given by the workmen out of the king's yard sent up by Sir William Penn, there is a good stop given to it as well at Mark Lane end as ours, it having only burned the dyall of Barking Church and part of the porch there quenched. I up to the top of Barking steeple and there saw the saddest sight of desolation that I ever saw'.

All Hallows is renowned for its fine brasses. You will find seventeen. The earliest (1389) is a memorial to William Tonge.

The sword rests in All Hallows are among the finest in the City.

In the Lady Chapel is the Toc H shrine.

The Worshipful Company of Mercers hold their annual service here. The Mercers are the senior Livery Company.

The Worshipful Company of Blacksmiths also hold their annual service here.

The Worshipful Company of Gardeners hold a flower festival here.

The Guild of World Traders also worship here.

The Grinling Gibbons font cover

LOOK at the very fine brasses.

LOOK at the sword rests.

If you look across Byward Street from the door of All Hallows, you will see Seething Lane. Cross by the subway, then walk up Seething Lane. On your right you will see some gardens (Samuel Pepys lived in a house here). At the end of the road on your left is St Olave.

Before entering LOOK at the stone skeleton heads set over the gateway. This entrance is sometimes closed, but if you walk round the church you will find another entrance in Hart Street.

St Olave Hart Street

Hart Street, London EC3.
Open: Monday-Friday 9-5, Saturday closed,
Sunday service 11am.
Nearest Tube: Tower Hill.

First mentioned in 1109.
Rebuilt in the middle of the 15th century.
Escaped the Great Fire.
Terribly damaged in the Blitz.
Carefully restored by Ernest Glanfield.

The dedication is to the Norwegian King Olave who died in 1030 helping Ethelred "the Unready" to expel Danish invaders. It is probable that there was an early church on this site. This church is one of the smallest in the City and has the feeling and appearance of a country church with a real churchyard, not a garden. This is entered from Seething Lane under a grisly looking stone gateway decorated with skulls and iron spikes. Charles Dickens called this "the gateway of St Ghastly Grim". There is another entrance to the church from Hart Lane.

A chrisom.

In the 14th century it was known as St Olave next the Friars of Holy Cross, as a monastery was built close by which survived until the reign of Henry VIII (1509-47). Its memory still endures in the name of the road nearby, "Crutched Friars". Surviving the Great Fire, it was practically demolished by bombs in 1941 but beautifully restored in the 1950s by Ernest Glanfield.

The St Olave that is always associated with Samuel Pepys was built in the 15th century. It is referred to frequently in his diaries. One entry reads: *"To our own church, it being the common fast day and it was just before the sermon, but Lord how all the people in the church stared upon me and see me whisper to Sir John Minnes and my Lady Penn. Anon I saw people stirring and whispering below, and by and by come up the sexton from my Lady Ford to tell me the news that I had brought, being now sent into the church by Sir W. Batten in writing and passed from pew to pew".* The news was that the English had just defeated the Dutch in a famous battle at sea.

The principal builders and benefactors were the brothers Richard and Robert Cely, whose memorials can be found near the altar. Conspicuous among the colourful monuments are two of plain marble to Samuel and Elizabeth Pepys. The memorial to Samuel Pepys was placed there in 1884. Every year at the end of May a special commemorative service is held. The register records his burial on 4 June 1707 in a vault under the communion table.

The Vestry House attached to the church dates from the time of Charles II and has a fine plaster ceiling and interesting furniture.

Trinity House hold their annual service here.

The Worshipful Company of Clothworkers hold their annual service here.

The parishes of All Hallows Staining and St Katherine Coleman are united with St Olave.

LOOK at the memorials to Samuel & Elizabeth Pepys.

LOOK at the monuments by the altar.

LOOK at the pulpit, which is well carved and came from St Benet Gracechurch Street.

LOOK at the fine stained glass windows in the Lady Chapel, noting the connection with the two churches united here.

GO DOWN to the Crypt, where you can see the remains of the earliest church.

The gate of "St Ghastly Grim"

Detail from Lady Chapel window.

To reach the tower of All Hallows Staining, go into Hart Street, walk across the forecourt of Fenchurch Street Station, look to your left and you can see the tower.

41

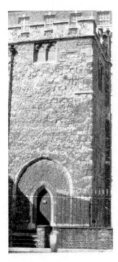

All Hallows Staining

Star Alley, Mark Lane, London EC3.
Nearest Tube: Tower Hill.

All that remains of this fifteenth century church is the tower. The church survived the Great Fire, but the body of the church fell down in 1671. It was rebuilt, but finally pulled down in 1870. The parish was then united with St Olave Hart Street.

The word Staining (made of stone) distinguished it from the other All Hallows churches, which were built of wood.

When the parish united with St Olave, all its treasures were given to St Olave with the exception of the sword rest, which went to St Andrew Undershaft, (see Walk 1).

The church bell was sent to Grocers' Hall. It is the oldest bell in the City and was made in 1458. It is still there.

St Katherine Coleman

To reach the garden of St Katherine Coleman, (demolished in 1925), go back into the forecourt of the station, turning left past the station along Railway Place, a short road. Turn right, walk a few yards to St Katherine's Row, and you will see the beautiful garden of St Katherine Coleman.

To reach St Margaret Pattens, walk back along Fenchurch Street and take the fifth turning on your left, Rood Lane. At the bottom on the left is St Margaret

St Katherine's Row, London EC3.
Nearest Tube: Tower Hill.

First mentioned in 1301, the dedication was to St Katherine and All Saints. "Coleman" was either a builder or a benefactor. The church escaped the Great Fire and was repaired in 1703, but pulled down in 1734. A new church was built on the site, and it was confidently said that no other parish in the City would have erected such a piece of ugliness!. The last service was held in 1921. It was finally pulled down in 1925 and its parish united with St Olave Hart Street.

St Margaret Pattens

Eastcheap, London EC3.
Open: Monday-Friday 8-4.
Nearest Tube: Monument.

Mentioned in a charter of Henry I (1100-1135).
Rebuilt in 1538.
Destroyed by the Great Fire.
Rebuilt by Sir Christopher Wren in 1687

The name signifies dedication to St Margaret of Antioch, a virgin and martyr at the end of the 3rd century. The origin of the word "Pattens" has been the subject of much discussion over the centuries. Pattens were wooden clogs or overshoes, and the church was situated in an area occupied only by makers of and dealers in pattens. In the vestibule is the following notice: "*Will the women leave their pattens before entering the church, and the men wipe their shoes on the mat!*" The name of the lane was changed from St Margaret Pattens Lane to Rood Lane at the time of the rebuilding of the church in 1538. A cross (or rood) was erected in the grounds. Those who came to pray before it and contribute to the rebuilding costs were blessed by the Pope and their sins pardoned! Soon after the Reformation the rood was pulled down and secretly destroyed. Following the Great Fire the parish of St Gabriel Fenchurch was united with St Margaret.

The church has a lofty medieval-looking spire, 200 feet high, but not as high as either St Bride or St Mary le Bow.

Sword rest and lectern in St Margaret Pattens

As you enter the church from the vestibule you will notice the two canopied pews on either side of the door, reserved for churchwardens. Between these pews are to be seen the arms of James II (1685-1701), the only example of his arms in the City. Sir Christopher Wren was believed to have worshipped here regularly and his monogram in inlaid wood is to be found in the pew on the south side. On one of the pews you will see a carved lion and on the other a unicorn.

The reredos contains a painting by the seventeenth century Italian painter Carlo Maratti, and the altar piece has carvings of the

LOOK at the two canopied pews.

SEE the arms of James II.

43

LOOK at the Punishment Bench.

Look at the memorial to Charles I.

LOOK at the font.

In the Lady Chapel are a fine 17th century chair and stool. They came from St George Botolph Lane.

A boxed pew

To reach the next church, St Dunstan in the East, of which only the tower and body of the church remain, cross Eastcheap, turn left, take the next right turning. Idol Lane and St Dunstan is on the left. Do walk in to see the remains. It is well worth your visit.

Grinling Gibbons school. On the left of the altar is the beadle's pew, and next to it is the 'Punishment Bench', with a carved devil's head. This bench was for children who did not behave themselves during the service.

The copper cross on the south wall (it was at one time on the spire) is a copy of the one on St Paul's Cathedral. Beneath it is a memorial to the King and Martyr, Charles I (1625-49). There used to be a special service here for Charles I on 30th January.

St Margaret is fortunate to possess a fine sword rest. This was given by Sir Peter Delme, a former Governor of the Bank of England and Lord Mayor. It is unusual in that it has four shields. Can you identify them? They are the Royal Arms, the City Arms, the Fishmongers' and those of Sir Peter Delme.

Look carefully at the font. The fine carving is said to be by Grinling Gibbons, but not the cover. Beyond this are a few examples of old tapestry, one from Bruges in Belgium.

There is a shrine to a naval officer who died in a submarine accident in 1918.

St Margaret Pattens is now a Guild Church.

St Margaret Pattens,
James II coat of arms beneath the organ

St Dunstan in the East

Idol Lane, London EC3.
Nearest Tube: Monument.
Nearest Public Toilets: Monument Street.

Stow said that this was a *'fayre and large church of an ancient building and within a large churchyard, and that many rich merchants, salters and ironmongers lived in the parish'.*

St Dunstan was destroyed in the Great Fire and then rebuilt by Sir Christopher Wren. By 1810 the body of the church was in a very bad state and had to be rebuilt. During the Second World War it was badly damaged in the Blitz, and today only the shell, tower and steeple remain.

On Easter Day in 1417 there was a terrible fight in the church. The wives of Lord Strange and Sir John Tussell had quarrelled. Their servants fell upon one another in the aisles, many were wounded and one man was killed. As a result the church was closed and those responsible were excommunicated. Lord and Lady Strange were ordered to appear before the Archbishop in St Magnus the Martyr and then in St Paul's. Lady Strange was ordered to offer the sum of £10 to found a Trust Fund for the orphans of the dead man, and Lord Strange the sum of £5. With other gifts collected a sum in excess of £100 was handed over to the City Chamberlain in trust for the orphans.

Today a wonderful garden has been created in the remains of the body of the church. Fine climbers wander all over the walls, and the foliage hangs like tapestries around the paneless windows. In the centre of the nave is a fountain washing over a stone base. Around this area benches face towards the East end, where the altar once stood. The whole atmosphere is one of peace and tranquillity. This garden is without doubt the finest in the City.

The walk to St Mary at Hill is very short. Go across Idol Lane and turn right into St Dunstan's Lane, cross over St Mary at Hill, turn left into the alley under the clock. Walk through the alley into Lovat Lane, turn right and after a few yards the entrance to the church is on your right.
Alternatively keep walking under the clock and take the second alley on the left, bringing you to the churchyard and another entrance.

St Mary at Hill

Eastcheap, London EC3.
Open: Monday-Friday 11-4.
Nearest Tube: Monument.

First mentioned in 1177.
Damaged in the Great Fire.
Rebuilt by Sir Christopher Wren.
Tower rebuilt in 1780.
Altered in 1826
Damaged by fire in 1988.
Restoration in progress.

This beautiful little church, first mentioned in records in 1177, was, until the fire of 1988, one of the City's least spoilt churches. One of its many charms lies in finding it, as it is tucked away down Lovat Lane with the entrance under the tower. In the narrow streets around the church you have a very good idea of how the City looked in the 1800s. Looking up towards St Margaret Pattens and down to where Billingsgate Fish Market once stood, it will be appreciated that the City lies on a steep hill

Damaged in the Great Fire, it was rebuilt by Wren. Considerable alterations and restoration were made in the 19th century. In 1967 the church was closed while an extensive programme of repairs and cleaning was carried out. This included removing much of the Victorian stained glass windows which darkened the church and about which M V Hughes, writing on the church in 1932, complained so bitterly. The windows now contain a mixture of sparkling new and 18th century glass. They give the light a special luminous quality which enhances the decorated ceiling and walls. This makes one forget for a moment that the famous box pews and wood carving are temporarily absent.

Much of the wood carving for which the church is famous was done by Wren's craftsmen. The talented Victorian woodcarver, William Gibbs Rogers (see Walk 2, St Michael Cornhill) was responsible for the pulpit, the lectern and probably the organ gallery. The organ was built in 1834 by William Hill of London.

Stow records that Thomas à Becket, who later became Archbishop of Canterbury, was appointed parson of "St Marie Hill". He also records a gruesome but interesting account of labourers digging the foundations of a wall in 1497 and finding a coffin of rotten timber. This contained the body of a woman buried over 100 years before, but her skin was still totally preserved and her joints pliable! It was the grave of Alice and her husband Richard Hackney.

The parishes of St Andrew Hubbard and St George Botolph Lane are united with St Mary. St George contributed two of the six sword rests found in the church.

At the end of the last century St Mary was threatened with demolition by plans to extend the railway, but it was saved by the City Church and Churchyard Protection Society. It was closed for two years for repairs and for the installation of electric light and reopened in state in 1894. During this time three thousand bodies were removed from the churchyard and reinterred in Norwood Cemetery.

The church has suffered grievously as a result of fire, most recently in October 1988 due to an electrical fault. It is being most carefully restored to its former glory under the ever watchful eye of the present Rector, Dr B.A. Kirk-Duncan, who is also the Hon. Archdeacon of Gambia in West Africa.

In these narrow streets you have a very good idea of how the City of the early 1800s must have looked. You will also appreciate that the City is on quite a steep hill

Public toilets:

Monument Street.

To find the next church, retrace your steps and walk down Lovat Lane into Monument Street. If you look to your right you will see the Monument to the Great Fire. Cross first over Monument Street and then, at the lights over Lower Thames Street, turn right and you will soon find St Magnus the Martyr.

St Magnus the Martyr

Lower Thames Street, London EC3.
Open: Tuesday-Friday 10-3.
Sunday service:11.
Nearest Tube: Monument.

Very ancient foundation. Mentioned in the time of William the
Conqueror (1066-87)
The first church to be destroyed in the Great Fire.
Rebuilt by Sir Christopher Wren in 1676.
Restored in the 1920s.
Damaged in the Blitz. Post war restoration.

In 1067 the church is mentioned in confirmation of a grant by
William I. Unusually for this early period it describes the church
as being made of stone. St Magnus was once on the approach
road to London Bridge, which until 1750 was the only bridge
across the Thames. The passage under the tower was created in
1760. This was the first church to be destroyed in the Great Fire.

There has been the usual uncertainty about the origins of the
dedication. However it is now generally accepted that the
dedication is to a Norwegian saint, St Magnus, who was killed in
the Orkney Islands and buried in Kirkwall Cathedral. His statue
was placed in the church in 1924. It shows him holding a model
of the church.

One of the many famous and interesting people connected with
this church is Henry Yeule. He was master mason to three
monarchs: Edward III (1327-1377), Richard II (1377-1399) and
Henry IV (1399-1413). One of the buildings he worked on was
Westminster Hall. He was buried here in 1400. Miles Coverdale,
who produced the first complete English Bible, was reburied
here; his body was removed from St Bartholomew by the
Exchange when it was demolished in 1840.

This fine church is quite different in character from the other
City churches, and there is much to look at here. Spend a few
minutes and look carefully at the many fine and interesting details.

They include a fine altar piece, Queen Anne's (1702-17)

monogram on the gallery, and a very fine sword rest, also with Queen Anne's monogram, which has six shields. The font, given in 1683, is marble with an oak cover. Notice also the Russian icon on the north wall. There are also two fine chests dated 1614 and 1670.

The table of Benefactions in the lobby is well worth reading. It gives an account of the narrow escape of the church from a fire on London Bridge in 1633. To commemorate this a special sermon is given each year in February. Unfortunately it did not escape in 1666! In 1760 there was yet another fire, which caused a considerable amount of damage.

ASK if they still have the tobacco box and Falstaff Cup that came from St Michael Crooked Lane.

The church is recalled with poignancy by T S Eliot in the poem "The Waste Land".

The Worshipful Company of Fishmongers hold their annual service here.

When you leave the church, walk past and go round the other side, the river side. There is a small garden and a pathway to the river's edge, well worth the short walk.

LOOK at the fine Altar.

SEE the Russian icon.

READ the table of Benefactions.

LOOK at the sword rests with Queen Anne's monogram.

SEE the splendid model of the medieval London Bridge in the vestibule.

Pew end

Pelican in piety

All that remains of the next church, St Martin Orgar, is a tower. To reach it cross back over Lower Thames Street, walk up Fish Street Hill by the Monument, turn left and at the junction cross over King William Street by the subway. Now take the first turning on the left, Martin Lane.

49

St Martin Orgar

Martin Lane, London EC3.
Nearest Tube: Monument.

Earliest reference in the twelfth century.

The dedication is to St Martin of Tours (see Walk 6, St Martin Ludgate Hill). For the explanation of the name Orgar see St Clement Eastcheap (Walk 2) with which it is joined.

Stow says that the Church of St Martin Orgar is a small thing!

Part of the nave and the tower escaped the Great Fire.

The French Protestants used to meet here until 1820, when the building was dismantled, leaving only its tower, which was pulled down later.

The tower and clock that are seen today were built to mark the site of the church. The building is now offices, with their central heating system installed in the tower! The remaining churchyard at the side of the building must be the most desolate and uncared for of all the City churches' grounds.

Public toilet: At the junction of Upper Thames Street and Suffolk Street.

To reach St Michael Paternoster Royal, turn left leaving the tower that once was St Martin Orgar, and walk down the hill. Turn right into Upper Thames Street Continue walking, passing under a bridge (Canon Street Station) turn right into Dowgate Street and then left into College Street, the church is on your right.

50

St Michael Paternoster Royal

College Street, London EC4.
Open: Monday-Friday 9-5.
Nearest Tube: Cannon Street.

First mentioned in 1218.
Rebuilt by Sir Richard Whittington in 1400.
Destroyed in the Great Fire.
Rebuilt by Edward Strong in 1694 under the supervision of Sir Christopher Wren.
Damaged in 1944 by a flying bomb. Restored in 1968.

The church was first known as St Michael Paternosterchierch, but by the 1360's it was called St Michael in the Riole. Both "Riole" and "Paternoster" were names of ancient thoroughfares. Royal is a corruption of the name Reole, a small town near Bordeaux, from which wine merchants imported their wine. College Street was at one time known as Riole, and Queen Phillipa, wife of Edward III (1327-1377), had her wardrobe here. The area around the church is known as Vintry, the centre of the wine trade, another connection with Reole and Bordeaux.

LOOK at the brass candelabra.

This was the church of Sir Richard Whittington, a wealthy merchant and four times Lord Mayor of London; a household name in his own day due to his good works, in modern days immortalised forever in pantomime. He lived in a mansion nearby and in 1400 paid for the rebuilding of the church and made it collegiate. He died in 1423 and was buried here; in fact he was buried three times, but now the whereabouts of his grave are unknown.

LOOK at the modern stained glass windows.

All Hallows the Great, demolished in 1893, provided some of the woodwork, two carved figures and the magnificent brass candelabra for St Michael. This hangs from a lofty ceiling, painted a brilliant blue. The pulpit and sounding board have some excellent carving and are from the school of Gibbons. There are some fine sword rests; one was for the Lord Mayor's sword. Over the altar are three outstanding modern stained glass windows by John Hayward.

At one time an unusual event was held here on St Christopher's Day, 25th July, when cars would come to be blessed.

The Gold and Silver Wyre Drawers' Company hold their annual service here and the Vintners come in alternate years. The Vintners used to walk in procession, with the servants of the Company proceeding them, sweeping the street because of the unhygienic conditions of the City in mediaeval times! This custom is a reminder of Sir Samuel Pennant, Lord Mayor, whose monument is in the church. He died in an epidemic of jail fever in 1750, which also killed 60 other people having business in the same court. The tradition of placing herbs in the prisoner's dock to ward off sickness dates from this time.

Like many of the City churches, St Michael was almost concealed by the houses and shops built around it. Now, as a result of the bombing during World War II, the church can easily be seen from Upper Thames Street.

St Michael is the centre of The Mission for Seamen.

Royal sword rest

To reach the last church on this walk, turn right into College Street and cross over Queen Street straight on up Skinners Lane, with the church on your left. To find the entrance of the church, when you reach the end of the lane turn left into Garlick Hill.

52

St James Garlickhythe

Garlick Hill, London EC4.
Open: Monday-Friday 10-4, Saturday closed,
Sunday service 10.30
Nearest Tube: Mansion House.

First church built in 1326. Destroyed in the Great Fire.
Rebuilt by Sir Christopher Wren in 1682. Damaged in the
Blitz. Restored in 1963. Damaged by a crane in 1991, which
closed the church for 18 months.

The dedication is to the apostle St James the "Great". His emblem
the cockle shell, a symbol of pilgrimage, is to be seen in the church.
It was first called St James near the Vintry, later St James by the
Thames. Stow states, rather obviously, that the second name was
because the church originally stood on the banks of the Thames
and that nearby garlic was sold. Perhaps more than any other
City church, St James was closely connected with the shipping
trade. On one side of Upper Thames Street is Queenhithe; this
wharf was once the chief landing place in London for foreign
goods and was the City's oldest harbour. Queen Isabella, the
French wife of King John (1199-1216), was given all the harbour
dues coming from the hythe. Those who evaded payment of the
dues often obtained sanctuary in St James. In appreciation they
presented a life sized metal effigy of the saint, brought from Spain.
Unfortunately during the Great Fire the legs melted. The top
half, which was for many years in the church, has now
disappeared.

St James is joined with several other parishes, and its full name is
"Saint James Garlickhythe with Saint Michael Queenhithe and
Holy Trinity-the-Less." St Martin Vintry, All Hallows the Less,
All Hallows the Great and St Michael Paternoster Royal are
joined to it.

A cockle shell, the
symbol of the
pilgrim.

The church has many historic treasures, one of which is a unique
silver font for private baptisms. It is hoped that soon a museum
in the church will display them.

The credence tables on either side of the altar are a moving

LOOK for the cockle shells, a reminder of pilgrims & the pilgrimage made to Compostella in Spain, where St James' body was believed to be buried.

LOOK at the glass chandelier, smashed by the crane in 1991 but remade.

ASK if the calcified remains of an unknown young man are ready for viewing. This is the reality of the myth that St James Garlickhythe has a skeleton in the cupboard!

memorial to the 54 young people who died in the sinking of the pleasure boat "The Marchioness " in 1993. They are made out of wood taken from the ship.

You may well wonder why this church was known as "Wren's Lantern". At the time that the little church was rebuilt it was hemmed in by many other buildings, making the interior dark. This difficulty was overcome by placing the windows right at the top of the building, allowing natural light to enter.

Over the clock was a figure of St James, which was destroyed during the Blitz but restored in 1988. There is a fine tower, which was perhaps a study for Wren's west towers of St Paul's.

This is also the headquarters of the Prayer Book Society.

Clock on the tower with St James above

If you now wish to do Walk 4, the first church, (St Mary Somerset) is only about 2 minutes away. Carry on along Upper Thames Street and just along on your right under the bridge you will see it.

Walk 4
Baynard Castle to Austin Friars

St Mary Somerset, St Nicholas Cole Abbey,
St Benet Paul's Wharf,
St Andrew by the Wardrobe,
St Mary Aldermary, St Olave Jewry,
St Margaret Lothbury, Austin Friars.

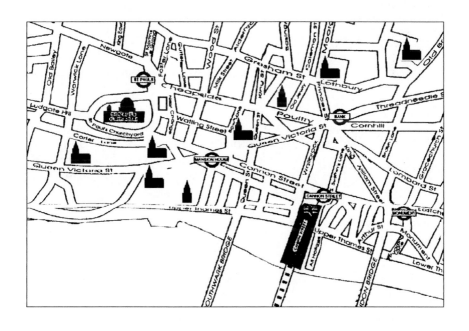

St Mary Somerset

Upper Thames Street, London EC4.
Nearest Tube: Mansion House.

First mentioned in 1170.
Destroyed in the Great Fire.
Rebuilt by Sir Christopher Wren.
Demolished in 1871, except the tower.

To start this walk the tower of St Mary Somerset must be reached from Mansion House tube station. Take the subway exit on your left from the station and then turn left again down Huggin Hill. A garden with a pergola will then be on your right. At the bottom of the hill turn right into Upper Thames Street and then first right into Lambeth Hill. Here, by the tower, you are at the start of the walk!

St Mary Somerset was first mentioned in 1170, but was destroyed in the Great Fire and then rebuilt by Sir Christopher Wren. The famous Bishop, Gilbert Ironside, was buried here. His name is perpetuated in the court behind the tower. As vice-chancellor of Oxford University he bravely opposed James II (1685-1688) to his face, as he upheld the rights of Fellows.

Nearest toilet:
By St Faith next to St
Paul's.

This was the first church to be demolished under the Union of Benefices Act of 1871, leaving just the tower standing in a small amount of churchyard. Alas it is no longer used as a meeting place for weavers of Brabant, who had been encouraged to settle here by Edward III (1327-77). The parish was united with St Nicholas Cole Abbey, just up the hill.

To reach St Nicholas Cole Abbey continue up the hill and cross over Queen Victoria Street, looking to the right.

St Nicholas Cole Abbey

Queen Victoria Street, London EC4.
Thursday 7 (prayer and Bible study),
Sunday 11 and 6.30 (services).
Nearest Tube: St Pauls.

First mentioned in 1144.
Destroyed in the Great Fire.
The first church rebuilt by Sir Christopher Wren after the
Great Fire
Gutted in the Blitz.
Post war restoration.

The church is first mentioned as Sancti Nichi Colabbei, and in
the 16th century as St Nicholas Wyllyms, perhaps after a
benefactor. The origin of "Cole Abbey " has never been resolved.
Stow calls it "Cold Abbey", which may be a reference to the
temperature! St Nicholas is the patron saint of children, travellers
on the sea and those confronted by sudden danger.

This part of the City used to be the centre of the fish trade and
the Worshipful Company of Fishmongers was associated with
the church. A bequest provided for a stone cistern set in the north
wall for washing fish. Further connections with the fish trade are
found in the early street names. Before Queen Victoria Street
was constructed, Old Fish Street led to the church. Friday Street
nearby recalls the days in Elizabeth I's reign (1558-1603), when,
in order to promote the fish industry, the Queen insisted that
everyone should eat fish on Friday.

The church was destroyed in the Blitz and many treasures were
lost. These included some of the finest carving by Grinling
Gibbons and the stained glass windows over the reredos, designed
by Burne-Jones. A few of the precious objects were recovered in
the ruins, including a fine candelabra, a sword rest, an early 16th
century painting of Jesus as a child and the 16th century lectern
from Rome. Post war restoration by Arthur Bailey closely followed
Wren's design.

To reach the next church,
St Benet, turn right into
the street and walk down
until you have almost
reached the imposing
building of the College of
Heralds; then cross over to
St Benet.

St Benet Paul's Wharf

Queen Victoria Street, London EC4.
Sunday services in Welsh.
Open: by special arrangement.
Nearest Tube: Blackfriars.

First mentioned in 1111.
Destroyed in the Great Fire.
Rebuilt by Sir Christopher Wren in 1683

The church was first mentioned in 1111 as Sancti Benedicti super Tamisiam and later in the 12th century as St Benedict by the Thames. Its full name now is St Benet Paul's Wharf. It was destroyed in the Great Fire but rebuilt by Sir Christopher Wren. Built of warm red brick and decorated with attractive white stone garlands over the windows, the exterior is one of the most unusual and attractive of the City churches. There have been many claimants for the title "Least spoilt of the City churches", but since the recent fire in St Mary-at-Hill (Walk 3) St Benet is now the leading contender.

The proximity of St Benet to the College of Arms and Doctors' Commons led to the burials of heralds and other dignitaries in the church. The College of Arms is still connected with the church. It is possibly the church referred to by Shakespeare in Twelfth Night, *"The bells of St Benet's, Sir, may put you in mind, said the Clown".*

Some of the famous people buried in the church are:

Inigo Jones, who was buried in the old church with his parents. There is now a small tablet set into the wall near his tomb.

Henry Fielding, married here in 1747 to his second wife, who had been maid to his first.

Elias Ashmole, antiquarian, (1617-1692), who was married to his first wife in the old church in 1638. His collections were given to Oxford University, where the Ashmolean Museum was established to house them.

The fine altar piece is made of oak and is surmounted by a circular pediment of inlaid woods. The supports are of angels in dark oak, and in the middle underneath is a figure of the Virgin and Child, almost hidden. Along the edge is an inscription carved in raised letters.

LOOK at the altar.

The parish was united with that of St Nicholas Cole Abbey in 1879, and St Benet was given to the Welsh Episcopalians.

As you come out of St Benet into Queen Victoria Street, you face the College of Arms. On your left across the road some way down is St Andrew by the Wardrobe.

St Andrew by the Wardrobe

Queen Victoria Street, London EC4.
Open: Monday-Friday 10-4, Saturday closed,
Sunday service 10.30.
Nearest Tube: Blackfriars.

First mentioned in a manuscript of 1244.
Destroyed in the Great Fire.
Rebuilt by Sir Christopher Wren in 1692.
Gutted in the Blitz.
Restored by 1961.

There has been a church on this site since 1244 and possibly even earlier. Because of its proximity to the nearby castle it was first known as St Andrew juxta Baynard Castle. Later in the 14th century it was known as St Andrew by the Wardroppe. The name of the church will seem strange to many people; it is so called because it was near to the office of the King's Great Wardrobe, which had previously been housed in the Tower of London. Thomas Fuller wrote this explanation in his book "The Worthies of England", published in 1662:

'There were kept in this place the ancient clothes of our English Kings, which they wore on great festivals, this Wardrobe was in effect a library for Antiquaries, therein to read the mode and fashion of garments in all ages. These King James in the beginning of his reign gave to the Earl of Dunbar, by whom they were sold, re-sold and re-sold'.

After the Great Fire the Wardrobe was moved to the Savoy.

In 1940 the church was damaged by incendiary bombs, but the walls and tower remained. Post war rebuilding was carried out in 1959-61. After the destruction of St Ann Blackfriars during the Dissolution, the parish was joined with St Andrew.

There was a monument to the famous Calvinist preacher, William Romaine (1714-95), in the Wren building. He often preached in the church, and his charismatic revivalist preaching attracted large crowds of people from all parts of London. The crowds were so large that they intimidated the churchwardens, who refused to open the church until the exact moment that the service began.

They also refused to light the church, so Romaine would preach by the light of a candle which he held in his hand. The fashionable congregations who followed him to St Andrew complained bitterly of the low kind of people in the area! One story tells of the day when the Bishop of London happened to see an unusually large crowd outside the closed door of the church; he enquired the reason. Some time later the Bishop appointed Romaine rector of the church, where he remained, continuing to attract huge crowds, for thirty years until his death in 1795.

In the 1930s an annual service was held here by West Indians.

Both the Parish Clerks' Guild and the Society of Apothecaries hold their annual services here.

A view of St Andrew by the Wardrobe

To reach St Mary Aldermary leave St Andrew by the back door, or go out around the door to the right. Walk up St Andrew's Hill, turning right into Carter Lane and keeping the Youth Hostel on your left, walk past St Paul's Cathedral and along Cannon Street until, on your left, you come to Bow Lane and the church. The entrance to St Mary Aldermary is down the alleyway at the side of the church.

St Mary Aldermary

Queen Victoria Street, London EC4.
Open: Monday-Thursday 1.00 subject to staff availability.
Nearest Tube: Mansion House.

First reference about 1080.
Rebuilt in 1510 by the Lord Mayor, Sir Henry Keble.
Burnt in the Great Fire, except the tower.
Rebuilt by Sir Christopher Wren 1681.

Tucked away behind a maze of medieval alleys is the oldest church dedicated to the Virgin Mary in the City. This can be understood from the early names. It was first mentioned in 1080 as St Marie Aldermarie and in 1272 as St Marie Eldemariechurche. It was burnt in the Great Fire, but rebuilt by the tireless Wren in 1681. The tower suffered in the great storm of 1703, but was eventually finished in 1711. Today the pinnacles are tipped with finials made in 1962 of golden fibreglass. The Victorians did their usual damage in the form of "restoration" in 1867, removing much of Wren's furnishing. However, the pulpit by Grinling Gibbons was preserved. The fan vaulting of the ceiling is the most striking feature of the church.

LOOK at the pulpit.

DO LOOK up at the wonderful ceiling.

Richard Chaucer, one of its benefactors, was buried in the old church in 1349. He was a forebear of the poet. Another poet, Milton, married his third wife here. Mrs Rogers, widow of a rich grocer, left £5,000, for its rebuilding after the Great Fire. An inscription over the door in Latin records this. A proviso in her will stipulated that the new church should look exactly like the old one.

One monument of medical interest is to a surgeon of St Bartholomew's Hospital called Pott. Amongst other things, he gave his name to a particular kind of fracture of the ankle which he sustained after being thrown from his horse in Southwark in 1756.

The church of St Antholin, destroyed in 1875, was connected with St Mary. The famous St Antholin Lectures, which were a feature of life in the medieval City, were given in this church for eighty years. St Mary Aldermary is now a Guild Church, with a particular interest in promoting retreats and the devotional life.

The fan vaulted ceiling in St Mary Aldermary

To reach the next church, retrace your steps and turn right into Watling Street, left into Queen Street and look right into St Pancras Lane, past all that remains of the churchyard of St Pancras and a blue plaque for St Benet Sherehog. Cross at the lights into Ironmonger Lane. Half way down the street you will see the tower of St Olave Jewry on your right.

St Olave Jewry

Ironmonger Lane, London EC2.

The earliest reference to this church is in 1181.
Destroyed in the Great Fire.
Rebuilt by Sir Christopher Wren in 1676.
Demolished, except for the tower, in 1888.

This tower, surrounded by a lovely garden, was once the home of the incumbents of St Mary Lothbury, and is now offices.

The brass weather vane, which you can just see, came from St Mildred Poultry.

To reach the next church on this walk, St Mary Lothbury, turn right as you come out of the garden, walk to the end of the street and turn right into Gresham Street. Cross over and turn to your right, but keep on the left hand side. At the traffic lights walk across Moorgate and you will see the church ahead of you on the same side.

St Margaret Lothbury

Lothbury, London EC2.
Open: Monday-Friday 7-7.
Nearest Tube: Bank.

First mentioned in the 12th century.
Rebuilt in 1440.
Repaired in 1621.
Destroyed in the Great Fire.
Rebuilt by Sir Christopher Wren in 1690.

St Margaret is situated immediately behind the Bank of England and incorporates other churches into its parish, as well as some of their treasures. The churches are:

St Mary Colechurch, destroyed in the Great Fire 1666.

St Martin Pomery, destroyed in the Great Fire.

St Christopher-le-Stocks, demolished in 1781.

St Bartholomew by the Exchange, demolished in 1841.

St Mildred in the Poultry, demolished in 1872.

St Olave Jewry, demolished in 1888 (the tower still stands).

St Stephen Coleman Street, bombed in 1940.

LOOK at the font and all the other splendid carving.

Commemoration of them can be found in stone medallions in the reredos.

The first mention of this church was in 1197, when it was referred to as St Margaret de Lodebure. It stands over the course of the Wall Brook, which was arched over at the expense of the then Lord Mayor, Robert Large. It was burnt down in the Great Fire, but completely rebuilt by Sir Christopher Wren in 1690. The font is of particular note and is carved with representations of Adam and Eve in Paradise, the return of the dove to Noah in the Ark, the Baptism of Jesus in the Jordan and the baptism of the eunuch by Philip.

The screen is a particularly fine one and was brought from All Hallows the Great. It was made in Hamburg and brought by the German Hanse merchants who originally settled here in 1250. They had their own Guildhall but no chapel and used to worship in All Hallows. Thus the area around Cannon Street was, until about the middle of the last century, a piece of Germany in England.

They enriched the church with many gifts besides the screen, including a candelabra and a pulpit and sounding board, which also went to St Margaret. St Christopher-le-Stocks' memory is preserved in two panels, representing Moses and Aaron, in the sanctuary. Even old (pre-Great Fire) St Paul's is remembered with the gilded cross in the Lady Chapel over the altar. This was made out of a piece of oak saved from the Cathedral that was destroyed in the fire.

To reach the last church in this walk, turn to your left as you leave. Walk along Lothbury and into Throgmorton Street. Carry on until you reach Throgmorton Avenue, walk down it, and on your right is Austin Friars. At the other end is the Dutch Church. At weekends Throgmorton Avenue is closed, so you continue to walk along Throgmorton Street and take the next turning on the left, Austin Friars. Then the church is just round the corner.

The interior of St Margaret Lothbury

Austin Friars Dutch Church

Austin Friars, London EC2.
Telephone: 0171-588-1684.
Open: Monday-Thursday 11-3. Ring bell at No 7.
Services Sunday at 11.
Nearest Tube: Bank.

The Monastery of the Augustinian Friars, founded in 1253.
Larger church built in 1354.
Severely damaged by fire in 1870.
Destroyed in Blitz in 1940.
Rebuilt 1950-56 by Arthur Bailey.

The Monastery of the Augustinian Friars (the Order of St Augustine of Hippo) was founded here in 1253 by Humphrey de Bohun, Constable of England, on his return from a crusade. In 1354 a much larger church was built for the monks by one of his descendants. During the Peasants' Revolt in 1381, Wat Tyler attacked the monastery, dragging out 13 Flemings from sanctuary and beheading them. Miles Coverdale, one of the monks, worked on his translation of the Bible here. After the Dissolution of the Monasteries under King Henry VIII (1509-1547) the buildings were given to the Marquess of Winchester. He used them as a storehouse and built a mansion nearby. His name is preserved in the surrounding streets.

In the early 16th century Protestants in the low countries, persecuted for their religious beliefs, fled to England, and many settled in London. They found refuge in a country where the King (Henry VIII) had recently broken with Rome, proclaimed himself head of the church and suppressed the religious houses. Their freedom of worship was confirmed in 1550 by a Charter of King Edward VI (1547-1553). The King also decreed that the former church of the Austin Friars should be used by the refugees for their services. After the death of the young King, his half-sister, Roman Catholic Mary I (1553-1558), ordered the Protestant refugees to leave the country. It was not until 1560, in the reign of Elizabeth I (1558-1603), that the church was restored to the Dutch Protestants. They have worshipped here ever since.

Austin Friars Dutch Church

Walk 5
Barbican via Guildhall to Bow Bells

St Giles Cripplegate, St Alphage London Wall,
St Alban Wood Street, St Mary Aldermanbury,
St Lawrence Jewry next Guildhall,
St Mary Staining and St John Zachery,
St Anne and St Agnes, St Botolph Aldersgate,
Christ Church, St Vedast alias Foster,
St Peter Cheape, St Mary le Bow.

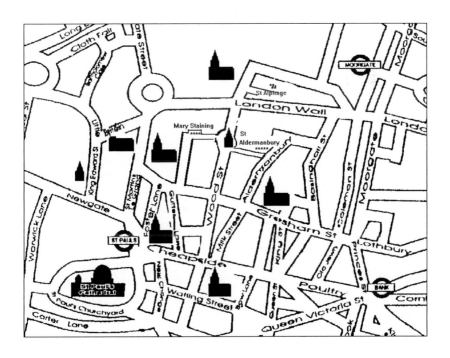

St Giles Cripplegate

Fore Street, Barbican, London EC2.
Open: Monday-Friday 11-4, services on Sunday.
Nearest Tube: Barbican.

First mentioned about 1090.   Rebuilt in 1357.
Largely destroyed by fire in 1545. Restored in 1858.
First City church to be damaged in the Blitz.
Post war restoration.

The dedication is to a Saint who was born of royal parentage in Athens. He was skilled in medicine as well as theology, but chose to live the life of a hermit in a forest in France. Legend says that one day when Flavius Wamba, King of the Goths, was hunting, his dogs pursued a hind into the Saint's cave. St Giles' prayers protected the hind, which in turn provided him with nourishment. This may be the reason why St Giles has always been associated with maternity, as well with the deformed and needy. The Saint and hind are portrayed over the porch of the present church. The interpretation of the last name of the dedication appears to be straightforward, especially as St Giles was always connected with the lame. However, the church was built by the City wall and a "crepel" means an underground passage connected to a fortified wall. This passage was sometimes used as a prison. A well once existed in the churchyard which was credited with miraculous cures for injured eyes.

There is a connection with St Bartholomew the Great (Walk 6) and its founder Rahere. His first almoner, Alfune, built St Giles in 1202. Nothing remains of that first church, except that in a recess under the tower is a piece of marble, which is said to have been the doorstep of the Norman church.

Fire was always a hazard for City churches and seems to have been especially unkind to St Giles, partially destroying it in 1545, when the London Chronicle reported as follows: *"Saturday 12th September in the morning, after five of the clock was St Giles church burned, bells and all".*

It narrowly escaped the Great Fire in 1666, but in 1897 the roof was badly burnt; then in 1940 during the Blitz it was bombed and burnt twice in one year. Like St Ethelburga (Walk 1), part of the church was obscured by the building of four small shops which existed until the beginning of this century. One of the buildings was known as the "quest-house", as it contained a "quest-room" used for parish and ward meetings. Much earlier in the church's history almshouses for the poor were built against the north wall by the Brotherhood of our Blessed Lady, or Corpus Christi, founded in 1362. These were sold after the Dissolution of the Monasteries. Nearby was the Jews' Garden, the only place appointed for the Jews to bury their dead in England until 1177.

The parish of St Giles suffered very badly in the Great Plague (1665). In one month the deaths filled 100 pages of the register.

There have been many Puritan connections with St Giles, one of the most distinguished being Oliver Cromwell, who was married to Elizabeth Bourchier here in 1620. John Milton was buried here in 1674. *"His funeral was attended by all his learned and great friends in London, not without a friendly concourse of 'the vulgar'. And there England's noblest poet was committed to the dust, calm in the Christian's sure and certain hope of a blessed immortality".* A cross in the chancel floor marks the spot.

A number of other notable people have been associated with St Giles. Sir Thomas More, the Lord Chancellor, (1478-1535) lived in the parish and worshipped here. Sir Martin Frobisher (1535-94) was an adventurer, who went on two expeditions to the Guinea Coast, the first when he was aged 19. He sustained fatal wounds in action off Brest and was buried in St Giles. Sir Humphrey Gilbert (1539?-1583), founder of Newfoundland, was also buried here. Daniel Defoe was born in the parish in 1660 and on his death in 1731 was buried here. Sir William Holman Hunt (1827-1910), the pre-Raphaelite artist, was baptised in St Giles. His most famous work, "The Light of the World", is in Keble College, Oxford. There is a copy of it in St Paul's Cathedral.

When you enter, the interior, now entirely uncluttered, gives the impression of space and tranquillity. Pews and the side galleries are gone. The Renatus Harris organ of 1704 was destroyed in 1940, but has been replaced by the organ from St Luke's, Old Street, made in 1733 by Jordan & Bridge. The organ loft sits well in the west end, and the glass doors in the base of the tower add to the feeling of spaciousness. St Giles forms a central feature in the Barbican, the vibrant centre of a business, artistic and residential community in the City of London.

Nearest toilets: In Barbican Centre.

To continue this walk, as you leave the church turn to your right and go round the corner into Wood Street, cross the road by the spot that marks the site of Cripplegate (Roman House) and turn left into St Alphage Gardens.

St Alphage London Wall

This is one of the 'invisible' churches.
St Alphage Gardens, London EC2.

The original building was an ancient Saxon foundation 1013.
Extensive repairs in 1624-49.
Escaped the Great Fire.
Taken down in 1774 and a new church erected in 1777.
Demolished, except the tower and vestry, in 1917.
Closed in 1920, (part of the tower and porch remained).
Completely burnt out in the Second World War.

Less than a stone's throw from St Giles is a lovely garden on two levels showing part of an old wall. This is all that remains of St Alphage. The Saint of the dedication was an Archbishop of Canterbury who was murdered by the Danes at Greenwich in 1012.

When you leave, turn left into Wood Street walk to the end, turn right and cross over Wood Street at the lights. Now cross right over the main road (London Wall). Straight ahead is the tower of St Alban Wood Street. To your right, but almost out of sight, is another little garden of the 'invisible' church of St Olave Silver Street.

The original church building became dilapidated in the sixteenth century. Opposite was Elsynge Spital, the hospital for 100 blind men, founded originally in 1329. At the Dissolution, this hospital, together with the Priory and all its buildings, was surrendered to the Crown. Part of this Priory church was pulled down, and dwelling houses built. The remainder of the building was converted into the new parish church of St Alphage. Some stones of the old original building could be seen up until the 1930s.

72

St Alban Wood Street

Wood Street, London EC2.

Very ancient origin.
Rebuilt by Inigo Jones in 1633.
Damaged in the Great Fire 1666 and repaired by Sir
Christopher Wren.
Destroyed in the Blitz.

The church is said to have been the chapel of King Offa, who
had a palace on this site. Only St Peter Cornhill can claim a
longer history. King Offa founded the Abbey of St Albans, and
there are several churches in London which belonged to it. The
church was gutted in 1941, then completely removed and now
only the tower remains.

St Mary Aldermanbury

Love Lane, London EC2.

On the left of the tower
is Love Lane. Walk down
the street and to your left
you will find one the
prettiest gardens in
London, protecting the
remains of St Mary
Aldermanbury.

The church was in existence in 1148. Aldermanbury derives its
name from the aldermen's hall. The church was partially rebuilt
in the 15th century by Sir William Eastfield, who presented five
bells for the tower. After being burnt in the Great Fire it was
rebuilt by Sir Christopher Wren in 1677.

It was damaged in the Blitz, and in 1960 it was dismantled stone
by stone and re-erected in memory of Sir Winston Churchill at
Westminster College, Fulton, Missouri.

Nearest toilet: Outside Guildhall Library.

The shell of the church after the Blitz

To reach St Lawrence Jewry, the next church, cross the road, and into Aldermanbury (passing the Guildhall Library), and at the end of the road you will see the church.

The church as it is today

74

St Lawrence Jewry next Guildhall

Gresham Street, London EC2.
Open: Monday to Friday 7-2, closed Wednesday.
Nearest Tube: St Paul's or Bank.

Burnt in the Great Fire. Rebuilt by Sir Christopher Wren.
Damaged in the Blitz.
Post war restoration by Cecil Brown in 1954-57.

The dedication is to St Lawrence, who was martyred in 285 AD.
At that time he was treasurer of the church in Rome, and was
ordered by the Emperor Valerian to produce all the church's
treasures. He assembled a crowd of sick, lame and poor people
saying, "Here are the treasures of Christ's Church". For this he
was roasted on a gridiron. This became his symbol and is found
in the old weather vane that crowns the church tower. The pattern
is echoed strangely in the modern television aerial farther down!
The word "Jewry," was an indication of the location of the first
church. It was built on the west side of the medieval quarter in
the City which was inhabited by the Jews. Although they were
expelled by King Edward I (1272-1307) the name remained.

Rebuilt after the Great Fire by Sir Christopher Wren, this was
considered to be one of his finest churches. It was united with the
neighbouring parish of St Mary Magdalene, Milk Street, also
burnt in the Great Fire but not rebuilt. Later it was united with
St Michael Bassishaw.

In the vestibule hangs a painting of St Lawrence's martyrdom,
thought to be by de Ribera ("Lo Spagnoletto"). It was first saved
from the Great Fire by a youth, who was rewarded with six
shillings. It was rescued again during the Blitz.

Angel of Glory

The medieval church also contained chapels of St Mary and St
James, but all that remains of the old church now is contained in
a glass cupboard by the north entrance. St Lawrence suffered
again in the bombing in 1940, and only the tower and the walls
remained. It was meticulously restored by Cecil Brown in
1954-57.

LOOK at the Wren window in the vestibule.

ASK if they still have the Steinway Concert grand piano, once owned by Sir Thomas Beecham.

ASK to see the rocking horse in the vestry.

The inside of the church is suffused with a golden light reflected from the gilding of the ceiling and tops of pillars and from the beautiful windows. The stained glass is a feature of this church. Wren's churches were traditionally built with large clear windows to let in all the light possible, and later builders and architects have often tampered with this concept at their peril. With the destruction of the windows and Victorian glass in the Blitz, the opportunity was taken in 1954-7 to restore the original pattern wrought-iron work. The coloured glass figures, designed by Christopher Webb, are set in the middle of the windows and surrounded by clear glass.

St Lawrence is associated with the City government more than any of the other churches, as the City Corporation is its patron. The Lord Mayor's pew is at the front on the right hand side, and other pews are designated for the Sheriffs and Court of Aldermen and Esquires. The Lord Mayor and Corporation attend the church twice a year in state: at Michaelmas before the election of the new Lord Mayor and in January before the opening of a newly elected Court. More reminders of the City's patronage will be found in the church: on the south sanctuary wall is the City flag, and the City coat of arms is on the choir gallery.

People of note connected with the church are:

Godfrey Bollen, mercer and Lord Mayor in 1457, and Thomas Bollen his son, who died in 1471. This spelling is a version of "Boleyn". The Lord Mayor was the great grandfather of Anne Boleyn, second wife of Henry VIII (1509-1547).

Sir Richard Gresham, Lord Mayor 1537, father of Thomas Gresham. He was buried in the same grave as his first wife, Dame Alice Avenson. She was an interesting lady of virtue and substance who had been married three times previously and was noted for her good work to the poor of the parish.

With your back to the church, walk along Gresham Street and on your right down Staining Lane you can see the garden of St Mary Staining. Also on your right is the garden of St John Zachery.

John Tillotson 1630-94, most renowned preacher of his age, Archbishop of Canterbury 1691. He was married and buried here.

The Worshipful Company of Goldsmiths hold their annual service here.

St Lawrence Jewry next Guildhall

St Mary Staining

Oat Lane, London EC2.

First mentioned as "Ecclesia de Staningehage" in 1189. It is suggested that its name means it once belonged to the ancient manor of Staines, included by Edward the Confessor (1042-1066) in a grant to St Peter's Westminster. It could also indicate that it was made out of stone, unusual in early times when buildings were often made from wattle and daub.

After the Great Fire the parish was united with St Michael Wood Street, and on its destruction with St Alban Wood Street.

St John Zachery

This attractive garden at the corner of Gresham and Noble Streets was first laid out by Auxiliary Fire Service workers in the Second World War. As a church its first mention was in 1181, when it was called St John the Baptist. In the 12th century it was granted by the Canons of St Paul's to *"Zacheries, so that he may visit the church regularly."* Hence the dedication. The church was destroyed in the Great Fire and united with St Anne and St Agnes, which is just across Noble Street.

To reach St Anne and St Agnes is only a few yards. Indeed you can see it from here.

St Anne and St Agnes

Gresham Street, London EC2.

Open Monday and Wednesday 10-4, Sunday for services.
Lunch time music "The best in the City".
Lutheran English- speaking services.
Occasional services in 13 different languages, including
Latvian, Estonian and Swahili.
Nearest Tube: St Paul's.

St Agnes is first mentioned in 1200.
St Anne de Aldredesgate is first mentioned in 1275.
Jointly mentioned in 1471.
Burnt in 1548.
Burnt in the Great Fire.
Rebuilt and reopened by Sir Christopher Wren in 1681.
Damaged in the Second World War.
Restored in 1966.

The dedications are to St Anne, mother of the Virgin, and St
Agnes a virgin martyr, who suffered in 304 AD. St Anne was
known in 1275 as St Anne de Aldredesgate and more romantically
as St Anne in the Willows, although Stow in his Survey of London
says that even at that time there were no willows growing there,
only ash trees. St Anne's church was said to be attached to the
famous or infamous collegiate church of St Martin le Grand.
The right of sanctuary there was so strong that even after the
church was demolished, sanctuary could be claimed simply by
standing on the ground.

For four years after the Great Fire the parishioners had nowhere
to worship, so they enthusiastically collected £160, made a
temporary church in the grounds and carried on their services
until the church was rebuilt. The neighbouring church of St John
Zachary was not rebuilt, and the parishes were united.

Although still owned by the Church of England, this is the centre
of Lutheran worship in England, which has an unbroken tradition
since German builders were brought in to help rebuild London
after the Great Fire. The church stands in a well kept garden of

LOOK at the Lion and Unicorn. shrubs and plants, seemingly flowering at all times of the year. The plain brick exterior hides one of the most attractive interiors of churches of the City of London. The church is wonderfully light and airy, due to large clear windows. Two paintings of Aaron and Moses are on either side of the altar, above which are panels with the Lord's Prayer, the Ten Commandments and the Apostles' Creed. The central dome is supported on four columns, on two of which are heraldic representations of the Lion and the Unicorn. There is much attractive gilded decoration, with cherubs' heads and leaves. One gilded angel stands over the entrance to the church and another supports the lectern.

Famous historical characters connected with this parish include the poet, John Milton, John Bunyan, author of 'Pilgrim's Progress', and John Wesley, who preached here twice a month.

The lion and the unicorn

To reach St Botolph turn right, walk the 50 yards into Aldersgate Street and turn right again. Over on the other side and a little further down is St Botolph.

St Botolph Aldersgate

Aldersgate Street, London EC1.
Open: Very infrequently.
Nearest Tube: St Paul's.

Founded in 1260.
Escaped the Great Fire, only slightly damaged.
Rebuilt in 1788 by Nathaniel Wright.

The exotic pulpit,
St Botolph

LOOK at the pulpit.

To reach the ruin of
Christ Church turn right
out of the church along
St Martin-le-Grand and
right into Angel Street.

The dedication is to St Botolph, who was at one time widely venerated throughout England as the patron saint of travellers. Thus dedications to him are found in churches at city gateways, quays and wharves where trade and goods entered the city. The church belonged to the dean and canons of St Martin le Grand. In the reign of Henry VII (1485-1509) it was given to the Abbot and Convent of Westminster. The Dean and Chapter of Westminster still appoint the rector. The Brotherhood of St Fabian and St Sebastian and the Brotherhood of the Holy Trinity in 1446 were founded in the church.

From the outside the church looks as if somehow it had been lost and forgotten long ago. It is rarely open, and when the opportunity to enter does present itself this same feeling pervades the interior. It possesses an elegant blue and white plaster ceiling, covered in circles of white leaves shaped like rosettes, with hanging tendrils on a blue background. The rest of the church is an unhappy mishmash of decoration and styles. The windows by the ceiling are attractive half-moons of leaded glass, but on the next level they are garish Victorian stained glass. Lighting the pews are windows of rather naive post-war coloured glass, which looks completely out of place. There is an elegant pulpit balanced on top of an ornately carved palm, but the marbling around the altar and the brown moulded curtains above, framing the east window, are hideous to behold.

The Worshipful Company of Plaisterers hold their annual service here in July.

Before going on to the next church look next door at the "Postmen's Garden" with its poignant memorials.

82

St Botolph Aldersgate

Christ Church

King Edward Street, London EC1.

First church built in 1325.
Re-founded in 1547.
Damaged in the Great Fire.
Rebuilt by Sir Christopher Wren (completed in 1704).
Destroyed in the Blitz.

In 1940 German bombs reduced the church to a shell. All that is now left to remind us of the magnificent building, over three hundred feet long and built by the Franciscan Friars in 1228, are the north walls and the vestry house, rebuilt in 1981.

Christ Church from the earliest times was richly endowed with money, materials and a library. Many famous people of the past were connected with this church, including Sir Richard ("Dick") Whittington, and it was the burial place of four Queens.

Once the site of the famous Blue Coat School, or Christ's Hospital, which was founded by the Franciscan Friars for fatherless children, the church is now left as an open space with shrubs and flowering trees.

To reach St Vedast alias Foster, retrace your steps along King Edward Street to the lights and cross into Angel Street. At the end of the street turn right into St Martin-le-Grand. Walk to the lights, then continue with St Paul's on your right, cross at the lights into Cheapside. St Vedast is in Foster Lane, the first turning on your left.

The demolition of part of Christ Church

St Vedast alias Foster

Foster Lane, Cheapside, London EC2.
Open: Monday-Friday 7-6, Sunday service 11.
Nearest Tube: St Paul's.

First mentioned in 1291 as Sancti Vedasti. In 1315-16 known
as St Fauster. In 1352 known as St Vedast and Amandus. (They
both share the same feast day, 6th February).
Rebuilt in 1519 and again in 1617. Damaged in the Great
Fire.
Rebuilt by Sir Christopher Wren in 1687.
Destroyed in the Second World War, except for the tower and
some of the walls. Repaired and re-hallowed in 1962.

A church has stood on this site since the 13th century and the
dedication is to St Vedast, Bishop of Arras, who died in 540 AD.
He was well known as a healer and performed many miracles
during his life. He is especially associated with diseases of the
eyes and children who walk with difficulty. It may be wondered
that such an obscure Saint should find his way to a City of London
church, but it is thought that, after the Norman conquest in 1066,
there was a Norman French colony in this part of the City.
Furthermore the Archbishop of Canterbury at that time had
expressly forbidden new churches to be dedicated to Anglo-Saxon
Saints. Various forms or corruptions of Foster are simply other
forms of Vedast, but there have been so many that eventually the
church became known as it is today under the unusual name of
St Vedast alias Foster.

Sir Christopher Wren's graceful tower, which is 160 feet high,
fortunately survived the Blitz, but is most sadly hemmed in by
modern buildings. The rest of the church has been rebuilt to
Wren's design.

The bells, cast in the Whitechapel Foundry, and rung every
Sunday, are said to be the sweetest sounding in the City. The
seating was arranged lengthways for more intimacy in the
collegiate style, and the only lighting is from small shaded lights
at the end of each pew. The white and gold plaster ceiling,
wreathed with silver, is similar to that of St Clement (Walk 2).

86

Over the sanctuary the Holy Spirit appears in the form of a dove. The chapel is dedicated to Our Lady and St Dunstan, who was the patron saint of goldsmiths (their Livery Hall is nearby). However, this is the church of the Worshipful Company of Saddlers, who hold their annual service here each July, just before the election of a Warden.

The font and the Lord Mayor's sword rest came from St Anne and St Agnes. The pulpit came from All Hallows Bread Street and is believed to be by Grinling Gibbons. The pulpit has a new panel showing the church in the Blitz with the bells falling from the belfry. The restoration is shown with a phoenix rising from the ashes.

LOOK at the phoenix on the pulpit.

The stained glass windows are modern but those in the chapel are made up from fragments of other windows, collected after the bombing.

LOOK at the windows in the chapel, made from fragments of other windows, collected after the bombing.

Persons of historical interest connected with this church are: Thomas Pelham Dale who was brought before the Court of Arches (see St Mary le Bow the next church) for "ritualistic practices"; Robert Herrick the poet, who was baptised here in 1591: and another poet, Sir John Betjeman, who was one of the first churchwardens after the rebuilding in 1962.

Next to the church is Fountains Court, so called because an Inn of that name stood here before the rectory was built. Under the gallery is a stone with cuneiform text on it. Canon Morrlock, rector 1947-67, spent a year excavating in the middle east with Agatha Christie and her husband Sir Max Mallowan. When the restoration was started, the Syrian Government sent the stone to be incorporated into the building.

13 parishes are united with St Vedast, St Michael le Querne, St Alban Wood Street, St Matthew Friday Street, St Olave Silver Street, St Peter Cheape, St Michael Wood Street, St Mary Staining, St Michael Bassishaw, St Leonard Foster Lane, St Anne & St Agnes, St Mary Magdalene Milk Street, St John Zachery, St Mary the Virgin Aldermanbury.

To reach the last church on the walk, retrace your steps into Cheapside turning left and pausing to look on your left. After the second bus stop and behind a shop, you will see a large tree set in the remains of the churchyard of the "invisible" church of St Peter Cheape, Wood Street.

The carved pulpit of St Vedast alias Foster

Glory in St Vedast alias Foster

St Peter Cheape

Wood Street, Cheapside, London EC2.

First mentioned in the 15th century.
Burnt in the Great Fire 1666 and never rebuilt.

Thomas Wood, a London Sheriff in the year 1491, was a benefactor of the building of St Peter Church. John Shaa (Shaw), a goldsmith, who died in 1503, left instructions in his will for a steeple to be built on St Peter. However it was Thomas Wood who was considered to be the main benefactor of the church because the rood of the middle aisle was supported by figures of woodmen!

Retrace your steps and on the other side of the road is the last church in this walk, St Mary le Bow.

St Mary le Bow.

Cheapside, London EC2.
Open: Monday-Friday 6.30-6.
Dialogues: Tuesday 1.05.
Nearest Tube: St Paul's.

Ancient foundation.
Roof blown off in 1091; the steeple collapsed in 1271.
Destroyed in the Great Fire.
Rebuilt by Sir Christopher Wren (completed in 1680).
Destroyed in the Blitz. Rebuilt in 1964.

The foundations of the church are built on the remains of a Roman basilica. The church is first mentioned in 1091 as Ecclesia sanctae Mariae quae dicitur ad Arcus, meaning the Church of St Mary which is called at the Arches (or Bows). There are the usual conflicting reports to be found about the true origin of the name, "arcus" meaning both arch and bow in Latin. One source says that during the reign of William the Conqueror (1066-87) it was the first church to be built on stone arches. Another version attributes the name to the arches in the steeple, so there is a choice! The gallery over the porch was built by Wren to commemorate the ancient structure put there by King Edward III (1327-77) in order that he and Queen Phillipa could watch the jousting. The Chepe was a large open market area where frequent pageants were staged.

A unique ecclesiastical court, the Court of Arches, is still held in the crypt. Bishops of the Province of Canterbury have their election confirmed here before an audience with the Sovereign.

St Mary le Bow has a history of rather sensational damage in storms. In 1091 the roof blew off in what appears to have been a violent wind storm, killing several people. In 1271 part of the steeple fell down killing yet more parishioners. The steeple was a well known landmark, and lanterns were lit in it as a guide to travellers .

Often people evading the law sought sanctuary in churches. In 1284 a man accused of wounding another took refuge here but was discovered and killed. This act resulted in the hanging of 16 men, despite contemporary accounts blaming a woman called

Alice! She did not escape and was burnt. The church was closed, the door and windows being blocked up with thorns until it was reconsecrated. The curfew was rung on the bells of St Mary le Bow.

The celebrated "Bow Dialogues" have been a feature of the church's activities for over 30 years. The rector invites distinguished guests, from diverse backgrounds, to participate in a 40 minute discussion, conducted from two pulpits. This takes place weekly, and is usually attended by more than one hundred people.

The Worshipful Company of Grocers hold their annual service here or at St Stephen Walbrook. The Master of the Company decides each year. The Worshipful Company of Arbitrators is also connected with St Mary le Bow.

LOOK at the dragon weather vane.

In the 1920s it cost 2½p to go up the tower now it costs slightly more!

St Mary le Bow

Walk 6
Smithfield via Temple to Ludgate Hill

St Bartholomew the Great,
St Bartholomew the Less,
St Sepulchre without Newgate, The City Temple,
St Andrew Holborn, St Dunstan in the West,
Temple Church,
St Bride, St Martin within Ludgate.

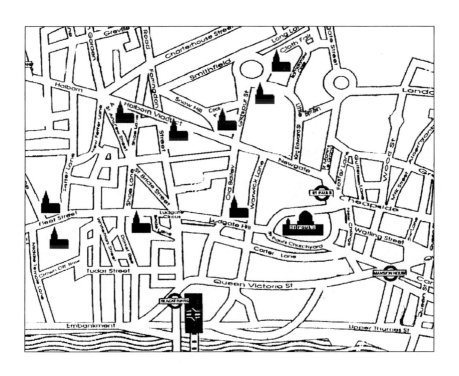

St Bartholomew the Great

West Smithfield, London EC1.
Open: Monday closed, Tuesday -Friday 8.30-5,
Saturday 10.30-1.30, Sunday 8-8 closed 1-2.30.
Closed Mondays in August.
Nearest Tube: St Paul's.

Founded by Rahere in 1123.
Great alterations carried out 1622-28.
Escaped the Great Fire.
Restored 1860-1910 by Sir Aston Webb.
Undamaged in the Second World War.

The dedication of this church is to St Bartholomew, one of the apostles. He preached in India and converted a Rajah's daughter to Christianity. For his pains he was flayed alive, and a flaying knife remains as his emblem. The word Smithfield comes from smoothfield, which in medieval times was a large grassy area.

Rahere, the founder of this church, was a courtier and minstrel to Henry I (1100-1135). Repenting of his frivolous life, he made a pilgrimage to Rome and whilst there was taken ill. Rahere made a vow that if he recovered he would build a hospital for the poor. He did recover, and during his convalescence St Bartholomew appeared to him in a dream, telling him to build a hospital at smoothfield. The connection between St Bartholomew and medicine was that the original hospital of St Bartholomew in Italy was supposedly founded by Aesculapius, God of Health.

LOOK at the tomb of Rahere.

The church was consecrated in 1123, and Rahere was the first Prior and Canon living under the rules of the Canons Regular of St Augustine. Many miracles were recorded during his life. He died in 1143. You can see his splendid tomb on the north side of the sanctuary. He is clad in the black habit of the Augustinian Canons, whilst at his feet is an angel with a crowned head. At the time of his death the choir had been completed, so we see it today as he would have seen it. Rights of sanctuary were granted to St Bartholomew, but later repealed by Richard III (1483-85).

Henry II (1154-1189) granted to the priory of St Bartholomew the privilege of holding a yearly cloth fair on 24th August, which lasted for three days. Trades people came from all over England to take part. Their booths were set up within the churchyard, which was surrounded by walls and gates.

These were locked at night and a watch was placed to protect the goods. During the day people flocked to see theatricals and side shows, and it became a carnival. In time merchants found other outlets for their goods and the fair became one of pleasure alone. Riots took place on 1st May 1517 in the City near St Andrew Undershaft (Walk 1), with the result that the fair was banned by the authorities and now remains a piece of history, commemorated in the name of the adjoining street, Cloth Fair.

In 1539, as a result of the Dissolution of Monasteries, the last Prior, Robert Fuller, surrendered the entire property to Henry VIII (1509-1547) and was granted a pension for life. To salve his conscience the King allowed the choir and transepts to serve as a parish church.

Candlestick

As usual, over the centuries much needed renovation and repairs have been carried out, sometimes at the expense of parishioners bent on "beautifying" their church. However from the years 1819-1906 three rectors should be particularly remembered for their tireless efforts and the use of their own money. They are John Abbis, William Penckridge and Sir Borradail Savory. Sir Aston Webb (1849-1930) carried out much needed restoration and continued his work for over forty years.

Portions of the church had been used over the years for commercial purposes. The North Transept housed a blacksmith, whilst in the Lady Chapel first a printer and then a fringe manufacturer carried on their businesses. The Lady Chapel was also supposed to have been a private dwelling at one time, with the walls raised by 15 feet and papered! In the crypt there was a coal and wine cellar and two schools were also kept there at various times.

One curious custom that began in 1887 and continues to this day was started by Joshua Butterfield. He bequeathed some money to the Churchwardens and directed that every year on Good Friday sixpence ($2\frac{1}{2}$p) should be given to each of twenty four widows resident in the parish. The balance was to provide children with hot cross buns.

The following are some of the interesting people and events connected with this church:

William Hogarth was baptised here in 1697.

Benjamin Franklin worked in the printing shop in the Lady Chapel in 1724.

LOOK at the shrine for the Knights Bachelor.

Behind the altar is a shrine to the Knights Bachelor, who hold their annual service here.

The City of London Squadron of the R.A.F. have their battle honour standard here. They also have a special service in May each year.

The City of London Yeomanry Association hold their annual service on the last Sunday in October.

The Worshipful Company of Butchers hold their annual service in September, before electing their Master.

The five pre-reformation bells are all named after Saints: Bartholomew, Katherine, Anne, John and Peter.

Side view of St Bartholomew the Great

Nearest toilets: Opposite the church entrance.

To reach the next church walk over to the hospital and turn into the hospital main gate. You will find the church tucked away to the left.

Bridal couple in front of Rahere's tomb

St Bartholomew the Less

Smithfield Gate, London EC1.
Open: Daily 6am-midnight.
Sundays Roman Catholic Mass 4pm.
Nearest Tube: Barbican.

First mentioned 1150.
Rebuilt by George Dance the Younger 1793.
Rebuilt by Hardwicke 1823.
Bombed in the Second World War.

This was originally the church of the hospital. It was transferred to its present site in 1184 and then known as the chapel of the Holy Cross until the Reformation, when it became the parish church. It is the only hospital parish in existence and was founded in 1546. Now tucked away on the left after entering the hospital precincts, the cream walls are covered with memorials to doctors and others connected with the hospital. Over the altar is a window to the Virgin, decorated with lilies. A hand written note used to be pinned to the door outside, asking visitors to be careful not the let in the blackbirds anxious to nest in the church! There is a calm and peaceful atmosphere, and it is hard to believe that here in 1838 a sexton, in a fit of despondency, hanged himself.

LOOK at the window over the altar dedicated to the Virgin decorated with lilies.

LOOK at the monument to Thomas Bodley.

During the Peasants' Revolt in 1381 Wat Tyler was carried into the hospital by the Lord Mayor of London, Sir William Walworth after being mortally wounded. Inigo Jones, forerunner of Wren, as a son of a clothworker was baptised here in 1573. On the east end of the north wall there is a monument to Thomas Bodley, founder of the Bodleian Library in Oxford. He died in 1613 and is buried here with his wife.

In 1793 George Dance the Younger rebuilt the church by creating a wooden octagonal inside, but this decayed, and the church was completely rebuilt in 1825 by Thomas Hardwicke. His grandson, P. C. Hardwicke, remodelled the sanctuary in 1865. Bomb damage during the Second World War was repaired by Lord Mottistone in 1951.

It is not a long walk to the next church, St Sepulchre without Newgate. Turn left out of the hospital gate into Giltspur Street and walk until the junction with Holborn Viaduct and Newgate is reached.

St Sepulchre without Newgate

Holborn Viaduct, London EC1.

Open: Tuesdays and Thursday 12-2.
Nearest Tube: St Paul's.

First mentioned in 1173.
Rebuilt about 1450.
Badly damaged in the Great Fire.
Repaired by the churchwardens,
Damaged during the Second World War.

The church was originally dedicated to St Edmund (see Walk 2) and for a few centuries was called St Edmund without Newgate, or simply St Edmund. Sepulchre is a connection with the first crusade and the formation of the Order of the Knights of the Holy Sepulchre in the 12th century. The church then became St Edmund of the Holy Sepulchre, later to be abbreviated simply to St Sepulchre. However Stow and Swift refer to it as "St Pulchre's", and there was a fifth century saint named Pulcheria.

The medieval prison of Newgate was close to this City church. Across the road a plaque now marks the spot. In olden times prisoners who passed the church on their way to the gallows were LOOK at the organ by Renatus Harris.
given a bunch of flowers; and the great bell always tolled at the fatal hour for executions. The bells are "the bells of Old Bailey" immortalised in the nursery rhyme. Because of its situation near Newgate the church has always been associated with prisons and crime in literature. Shakespeare makes mention of its bell, and Dickens writes of the church in "Barnaby Rudge" and "Oliver Twist". Many of the City churches have unusual bequests associated with them, and St Sepulchre is no exception. Again there is a connection with bells: in 1605 Robert Dowe left £50 for a man to ring a handbell and say a prayer at midnight on the eve of an execution. Also there is a memorial in the church to Sir Richard Reeve, whose charitable bequest in 1702 provided education for children living in the parish. This charity continues to flourish today but embraces an extended area.

LOOK for the brass tablet to Captain John Smith.

Perhaps the most famous person buried in the church is Captain John Smith, Governor of Virginia, forever remembered for his association with Princess Pocahontas.

LOOK for the piece of stone from the church of the Holy Sepulchre, Jerusalem.

This magnificent church has the largest area of any in the City, being 150ft long by 162 feet wide. Badly damaged in the Great Fire, it was intended to have been rebuilt by Wren, but the parishioners could not wait and carried out most of the work themselves! In common with all the City churches, repairs have been carried out over the centuries, but between 1870 and 1880 the main body of the church was completely changed. It was again remodelled in the 1930s.

LOOK at the windows dedicated to Sir Henry Wood and Dame Nellie Melba, the opera singer.

One of the founders of the Cistercian order, St Stephen Harding 1109-31, is commemorated in the chapel on the north side.

The Music Memorial Chapel has fine stained glass windows dedicated to Sir Henry Wood, John Ireland and Dame Nellie Melba.

Part of the churchyard is a memorial garden for the Royal Fusiliers (City of London Regiment), and a chapel in the church is dedicated to their memory.

The Organ

To reach The City Temple turn to your right, walk along Holborn Viaduct and you will see it across the road.

100

St Sepulchre without Newgate

The City Temple

Holborn Viaduct, London EC1.
Open: Monday-Friday 9-5.Weekends usually open.
Nearest Tube: Chancery Lane (closed on Sunday).

Foundation stone laid in 1873.
Destroyed in the Blitz.
Rebuilt in1958.

In early times nonconformists had no fixed places of worship, but moved from one site to another. The first mention of such a meeting, held in Anchor Lane, Lower Thames Street, is in 1567. Meetings were often held in private houses, City Livery Companies lent their halls, and churches were also used, lent by sympathetic priests. In the records of St Michael, Crooked Lane (sold in 1831) is one such mention. On 15th May 1648 Thomas Goodwin sought "leave to adminster the Lord's Supper to his congregation".

In 1873 the foundation stone was laid for the City Temple, which was completed in one year. At the state opening the Lord Mayor was the Guest of Honour. Designed in a light Italian style, the church could hold 2,500. It boasted an enormous pulpit, partly of Caen marble, which was a gift of The City Corporation. Gutted by enemy action in 1941, the church was restored in 1954-58 by Lord Mottistone and Paul Paget. Between the time of the bombing and the restoration the congregation met in St Sepulchre.

The cathedral of the Free Churches

Nearest toilet: In Charterhouse Street opposite Ely Place.

Our next church, St Andrew is just one minute away set in a garden. Turn left, and you can see it on the corner.

St Andrew Holborn

Holborn Circus, London EC4.

Open: Monday-Friday 8.15-4.30.
Nearest Tube: Chancery Lane (closed on Sunday).

First mentioned in 971.
Rebuilt in the 15th century.
Escaped the Great Fire.
Rebuilt in 1686 by Sir Christopher Wren.
Damaged in the Blitz.

In a charter of King Edgar (959-975) there is mention in 971 of a church of St Andrew and the boundaries of the parish. This may have been on the same site as St Andrew Holbornestrate in the 12th century. In 1291 it was called St Andrewe Holburn. It is situated near Holborn Viaduct, which was built in 1866 to cross the valley of the Fleet, one of London's hidden rivers. Over this river once stood a bridge called Oldbourne Bridge, perhaps casting some light on the word "Holborn".

The church was rebuilt in the 15th century and escaped the Great Fire. Rebuilt by Wren in 1686, it was the largest of his parish churches. In the Second World War bombs destroyed the interior but it was restored and re-hallowed in 1961. The church is now a Guild Church and used as an administrative centre for two departments of the Diocese of London.

LOOK for Thomas Coram's tomb.

Amongst the famous names connected with the church are:

Thomas Coram, who started his work for abandoned children in Hatton Garden in the 18th century. His tomb is at the west end.

Thomas Chatterton (1752-70), whose burial is recorded in the parish register. The tragic young poet committed suicide at the age of 17.

William Hazlitt (1778-1830) essayist, who was married here. Charles Lamb was his best man and Mary Lamb a bridesmaid.

Samuel Wesley, father of John and Charles, was ordained here.

Sir Marc Brunel (1769-1849), who was married here. He was engineer of the first tunnel under the Thames and father of Isambard Brunel.

St Andrew Holborn

To reach St Dunstan in the West turn left, walk to the lights, cross St Andrew Street/Shoe Lane, turn left into New Fetter Lane, leading into Fetter Lane, and when you reach its junction with Fleet Street turn right. St Dunstan is on your right.

St Dunstan in the West

Fleet Street, London EC4.
Open: Tuesday 11-3, Sunday service 12.30.
Nearest Tube: Temple/Chancery Lane both closed on Sunday.

Ancient foundation first mentioned in 1185.
Rebuilt by John Shaw and his son John 1831-33.

The first mention of St Dunstan is in 1185. Later, in 1237, St Dunstan over against the New Temple passed to the Crown from the Abbot of Westminster. However, in 1386 it was administered by the Norbertine Canons of Alnwick Abbey in Northumberland. Following the Dissolution it was given to Lord Dudley. The church survived the Great Fire, which stopped within three houses of the church when miraculously the wind changed. However, the building was demolished in 1829. The church, in its present form, was begun in 1831, and consecrated in 1833. A flying bomb in 1943 caused some damage, but not enough to discourage two intrepid Londoners who were married there the next day.

The rather sombre exterior of St Dunstan in the West, situated in the heart of Fleet Street, belies its fascinating interior and gives no hint of the exotic services and people who find their way here to worship. Romanian Orthodox, Armenian, Coptic, Syrian and Indo-Syrian services are held here, as well as Lutheran, Old Roman Catholic and Nestorian, each with its own chapel.

The Anglican High altar and screen are of 17th century Flemish origin, and the four windows behind it represent Archbishop Lanfranc, St Dunstan, St Anselm and Stephen Langton with King John signing the Magna Carta. The magnificent Orthodox icon screen altar, which stands to the left of the Anglican altar, was sent from Romania in 1966. It was originally carved over a hundred years ago for the Monastery of Antim in Bucharest. Amazingly, when it arrived at St Dunstan it was found to fit exactly. With great luck, on the day we first visited the church a charming person appeared, who related many interesting stories, and showed us the treasures of the church. He unlocked a door in the screen to reveal the altar behind, an extraordinary mixture of exotic icons, pictures of patriarchs, spangled textiles and a 1930s sideboard.

St Dunstan's churchyard was the hub of the book trade in the 17th century, and books often bore the inscription "Under St Dunstan's Church Fleet Street". Milton found a publisher here for his "Paradise Lost". Izaak Walton's "The Compleat Angler" was also published here.

LOOK at the monument to the famous Hoare banking family. They have served St Dunstan for three centuries as churchwardens, and a member of the family is still serving in this capacity. Hoare's Bank is across the road.

The clock with the figures of the two giants and the statue of Queen Elizabeth on the exterior of the church both have a long and mysterious history. The clock was bought by the church in 1671. The wooden giants struck the hours and quarters, hitting the bells with their clubs and moving their heads. They attracted large numbers of people from all over London. When the church was rebuilt, the clock was sold to the Marquis of Hertford who had it installed in St Dunstan's Villa, Regents Park. It disappeared until after the Second World War, when it was found and restored to the church by the generosity of Lord Rothermere.

LOOK at the statue and clock, and find the other three statues below Queen Elizabeth.

Queen Elizabeth's statue, which dates from 1586, now stands regally over the vestry door. Originally set over the old City gate at the bottom of Ludgate Hill, it was given into the care of the church when the gate was demolished. It stood on the church until the rebuilding in 1831-33 when it was sold for the sum of £16 10s. It then lay forgotten for 6 years in the cellar of an old inn near the church. "The Times" of April 1839 reported its discovery and the placing of the statue where you see it today.

The Cordwainers, one of the oldest Livery Companies, founded in 1272, are connected with St Dunstan.

Sir Richard Hoare's memorial

To reach the Temple Church cross the road and go through the large wooden gates. However on Sundays the gates are closed and access to the church is not possible.

St Dunstan in the West.

Temple Church

London EC4.
Open: Tuesday-Friday 10-4. Wednesday 2-4.
Sunday services: 8.30, 11.15.
Nearest Tube: Temple (closed on Sunday).
Ancient foundation, first mentioned in the 12th century.
Restored by Sir Christopher Wren in 1681-3
Restored again by Robert Smirke in 1828.
Damaged by bombs in Second World War, but repaired.

The church really belongs to two of the four Inns of Court and can be considered as the lawyers' private chapel. It was built on an ancient foundation, believed to be the chapel of St Anne, but the dedication is to the Virgin Mary. An inscription inside the door states that on 10 February 1185 it was dedicated by the Lord Heraclius, Patriarch of the church of the Holy Sepulchre in Jerusalem. The church was founded by and for the Knights Templars. After the order was suppressed it passed into the possession of the Knights Hospitallers.

Oliver Goldsmith was buried in the churchyard in 1774.

Sir George Thalben-Ball was the organist for many years until shortly before his death in 1981.

The doorway is a fine example, although restored, of late Norman work. It is still composed mostly of its original Caen stone. Inside, the marble capitals, which support the rood, were mainly erected by Wren. Old prints show that the walls and ceilings were once magnificently decorated with religious designs in colours of blue, red and gold. The Temple Church is a "Royal Peculiar", which means that the Sovereign appoints the incumbent, in this case known as the Master of the Temple.

LOOK at the effigies of the crusaders.

Henry III (1216-72) wanted to be allowed to join the Knights Templars and be buried in the church, but this was not possible. The death of his infant son allowed him to fulfil this wish vicariously. He gave the baby's body to the church, and it is believed it was buried in the tomb of Sylvester de Everden.

The effigies of crusaders, which attract much attention, have been very much restored and moved over the centuries so that it impossible to say with any certainty where their original places were. They all lie with their heads to the east. Two perhaps date from the 12th century and the rest from the 13th century.

To reach St Bride, go back into Fleet Street, turn right towards Ludgate Circus until you reach Salisbury Court. There is a sign post here. You enter the church under a dark arch.

109

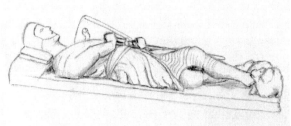

William Marshall, Earl of Pembroke
Temple Church

St Bride

Fleet Street, London EC4.

Open: Monday- Friday 8-4, Sunday for services.
Nearest Tube: Blackfriars.

First mentioned in 1222.
Destroyed in the Great Fire.
Rebuilt by Sir Christopher Wren in 1680.
Gutted in the Blitz.
Restored in 1957.

The church is built on the site of an ancient Roman cemetery, which was situated beside the main western thoroughfare out of the City. The dedication to the 6th century Irish saint, St Bridget, is rare among English dedications; possibly due to the early Irish and Norse settlers in this area.

The church has been called a "madrigal of stone" and is considered one of Sir Christopher Wren's finest works, after St Paul's and St Stephen Walbrook. It is one of the few churches whose windows look attractive from the outside. On entering the church the warm and intimate atmosphere, together with the natural light and sparkling interior, uplifts the soul.

Considering that St Bridget's tomb, in Kildare, was lit by an inextinguishable flame, it is not surprising that the church was consumed by the Great Fire. The steeple was once 234 feet high, but it was twice struck by lightning, giving Benjamin Franklin (see St Bartholomew the Great) inspiration to inquire into lightning conductors. The church was completely gutted by bombs in the Blitz and rebuilt in 1957. There are strong associations with the press; as St Paul Covent Garden is known as the actors' church, so St Bride is known as the journalists' church. They generously contributed to the post-war restoration. During the rebuilding, evidence of Norman and Saxon remains were found, and the crypt is now laid out as a museum. The bones from medieval burials are available for scientific study, and have already proved to be of great importance in many different fields.

There was once a well in the churchyard, which was reputed not only to have healing powers, but on the Saint's day a miracle occurred, turning the water into beer… small wonder that this is the journalists' church! Sadly nothing remains now of this wonderful well. Perhaps wells connected with City churches should be reinstated. The old well has also given its name to the English language as a place of detention. Henry VIII (1509-1547), rebuilt the old Norman fortified palace of Bridewell near the church to receive Charles V of Spain. Later his son Edward VI (1547-1553), allowed it to be used first as a hospital and then as a prison. Thus the name "Bridewell" meant a place of detention.

During the 18th century the view of St Bride from Fleet Street was completely obscured by many small shops, but a fire in 1824 removed some of them, and the view has been improved from the approach to the north door as you turn in from Fleet Street.

Samuel Pepys was baptised here at 8 days old in 1632, as his father lived near the church. Wynkyn de Worde, who took over Caxton's printing works, and the poet Richard Lovelace were buried in the pre-Fire church. Samuel Richardson was buried here in 1761, with his first wife and two infant sons. He achieved fame through his novel "Pamela, a moral tale written for guidance of life!" The Worshipful Company of Stationers, of which he was Master, erected a tablet to his memory on the north wall.

The last church on this walk is St Martin within Ludgate. To reach this church turn right into St Bride's Avenue and left into Bride Lane and right into Fleet Street, cross Ludgate Circus and go up the hill, you will see the church on your left.

Bluecoat boy and Charity girl

St Martin within Ludgate

Ludgate Hill, London EC4.

Open: Monday-Friday 10-4.
Nearest Tube: St Paul's.

Founded according to legend by King Cadwallon (985-986).
First mentioned in 1322.
Rebuilt in 1437.
Destroyed in the Great Fire.
Rebuilt by Sir Christopher Wren in 1684.

St Martin, soldier saint and Bishop of Tours, who died in 397, was famous for cutting his cloak in half to share with a beggar. Robert of Gloucester (1260-1300) states that the church was erected by order of King Cadwallon, who lived in the 10th century. However, the first actual mention is that in 1322 Robert de Sancto Albano was rector here. St Martin belonged to the Abbot and Convent of Westminster before the Dissolution of the Monasteries.

The church is situated half way down Ludgate Hill. A plaque formerly fixed to the church outside commemorated the site of old Ludgate, showing that the church was built on the old wall. Wren intended that the graceful leaden tower should be seen above the buildings. Unfortunately it is now almost hidden from view by ugly modern office blocks. The tower, if viewed from a particular point in Fleet Street, cuts the middle of St Paul's dome in half exactly.

LOOK at the Pelican of Piety.

St Martin was burnt in the Great Fire and then rebuilt in a cruciform shape with four columns. The font, as at St Ethelburga's (Walk 1) has a Greek palindrome taken from the church of St Sophia, meaning "Wash my sin, not my face only". A statue of the "Pelican of Piety" is in the baptistery behind the font. There are interesting pictures on either side of the altar. The three on the left are of St Mary Magdalene, St Martin and St Gregory.

LOOK at the fine carved doors.

113

In the church there is a monument to William Sevenoke, Lord Mayor in 1418, whose success story was similar to that of Dick Whittington. He was abandoned in the streets of Sevenoaks in Kent, and through the help of local people became an apprentice to a City grocer, later becoming a wealthy merchant. William Sevenoke later founded Sevenoaks School.

LOOK at the bell, given by William Warne in 1683, on the left of the Sanctuary.

There are wonderfully carved doors in the church: two to the right of the altar, one leading to the vestry, and one to the left leading no doubt to the garden at the side of the church where, the story goes, under a tree heretical books were once burned. The garden of Stationers' Hall, which divides the church and

LOOK at the fine double chair of 1690 with the churchwardens' names.

the hall, still boasts a huge plane tree. Perhaps it is in the same one. This church is one of the most appealing of the City churches. It cries out for a real congregation of all ages to worship here on Sundays, as in times gone by.

Just behind the church is a truly magical garden, well worth a visit. When you leave the church, turn left and after only a few yards you will find Stationers' Court. At the end of the court look to your left and you will see an archway, marked Stationers' Hall Office. Go through the archway, and there you have reached the magical garden.

Old Bell

114

NOTES AND BIOGRAPHIES

ADDISON, Joseph (1672-1719). English essayist, poet, leading contributor to and guiding spirit of the Tatler and Spectator. His skill as a writer led to important government positions.

BAYNARD'S CASTLE. Built by William the Conqueror in 1066. Headquarters of London's army until given to the Dominican Friars in the reign of Edward VI (1547-1553).

BEADLE. A parish officer appointed to keep order in church, punish minor offences, and give notice of vestry meetings.

BEDLAM. The hospital called St Mary in Bethlehem, used in 1547 as an asylum for the insane.

BENEFICE. The temporary right of property in an ecclesiastical estate. Derived from the Latin *"beneficium"*, which signified land granted to soldiers for faithful service.

BENTLEY, John Francis (1839-1902). Born in Doncaster, he was a pupil of Henry Clutton. He became a Roman Catholic in 1861, and started his practice as an architect in 1862. In 1894 he was appointed architect to Westminster Cathedral.

BLITZ. The bombing of London and other cities by the German Luftwaffe, from September 1940 to May 1941, early in World War II.

BRIDEWELL. From St Bride's Well, once a Norman fortified palace. It was given by Edward VI (1547-1553) to be used as a hospital; later converted into a prison.

BUTTERFIELD, William (1814-1900). Architect prominent in the Gothic Revival in England. Called the Oxford Movement's most original architect.

CHANTRY. A chapel, generally within a church, endowed by the founder for the singing of masses after his death. Begun in the 13th century.

CHIEF BUTLER. An officer of the Royal Court, who was responsible for the supply of wine to the Royal Table.

CHURCHWARDEN. One of the lay officers elected annually to help the incumbent with parish duties and to act as parish representative in matters of church organisation.

COLLEGE OF ARMS. Situated in Queen Victoria Street. It was built after the Great Fire (1666) by Wren on the site of a house belonging to the first Earl of Derby. It is the business of the College to deal with all matters of heraldry. The officers (heralds) are appointed by the Duke of Norfolk as Earl Marshal.

COLLEGIATE CHURCH. A church that is endowed for an associated body of clerics (canons and/or prebendaries).

COMPER, Sir (John) Ninian. (1864-1960). Church architect. Born in Aberdeen, Scotland. In 1882 he spent a year drawing at the Ruskin School in Oxford and then worked with church craftsman, C E Kempe. In 1883 he was articled to George F Bodley.

COURT OF ARCHES. The Archbishop's court held at the church of St Mary le Bow. A unique ecclesiastical court, held in the crypt.

COVERDALE, Miles. (1488-1569). Bishop of Exeter. Translator of the first English printed bible. Incumbent of St Magnus Old London Bridge (St Magnus the Martyr).

CROMWELL, Oliver. (1599-1658). English general and politician. Puritan leader of the Parliamentary side in the Civil War. He raised a cavalry force (called Ironsides) which helped to win the battles of Edgehill 1642 and Marston Moor 1644. He organised the Model Army which he led to victory at Naseby 1645. He declared Britain a Republic (Commonwealth) in 1649. Following the execution of Charles I, (1649) he ruled as Lord Protector.

DANCE, George the Elder (1695-68). His father, a mason, had come to work in the City of London where George Dance was born. He went into partnership with his father and in 1727 was co-architect with John Gould designing St Botolph Bishopsgate. Architect to the City of London, he designed the Mansion House.

DANCE, George the Younger (1741-1825). The youngest son of George Dance, who was surveyor to the City of London. Outstanding planner and designer, George the Younger was one of the original founders of the Royal Academy. His early training was in his father's office. All Hallows London Wall, was one of his churches.

DAPIFER. Title of the steward of a king's (or nobleman's) household.

DEFOE, Daniel (1660-1731). Born in Cripplegate, the son of a butcher. He was trained to enter the nonconformist ministry, but he became a hosier. He joined the Civil Service from 1695-99. He later became a writer and was sent to prison for his publication entitled "The Shortest way for Dissenters". He has been called the father of modern journalism He is, however, best remembered for his novel "The Adventures of Robinson Crusoe", published in 1719.

DOCTORS' COMMONS. Formerly a self-governing body of practitioners of canon and civil law, similar to the Inns of Court. Disbanded in 1858.

EVESHAM CHRONICLE. History of the Abbey of Evesham, written in three books. The second book, written by Abbot Thomas de Marleberge (Marlborough) in 1199, records the history and possessions of the Abbey.

FIELDING, Henry (1707-1754). Novelist, playwright and barrister, who, with Samuel Richardson, is considered the founder of the English novel.

FIRE OF LONDON. See Great Fire of London.

FOUNDLINGS. Children abandoned by their parents.

FRANKLIN, Benjamin (1706-1790). Printer, publisher, author, inventor and diplomat. Tenth son of a family of seventeen. When he was 12 he was apprenticed to his brother, a printer. He worked in printing in Philadelphia and London. He printed paper currency for the colony of Pennsylvania and later began the Pennsylvania Gazette. He invented the Franklin Stove, bifocal spectacles and the lightning rod. He was one of the diplomats chosen to negotiate peace with Great Britain after the American War of Independence.

GIBBONS, Grinling (1648-1721). Born in Rotterdam, his father was English. He settled in England and was encouraged by John Evelyn, who brought him to the attention of King Charles II, and Sir Christopher Wren. Gibbons was Master Carver to the Crown until 1721. He is buried in St Paul's Covent Garden.

GOLDSMITH, Oliver (1730-1774). Essayist, poet, novelist, dramatist and eccentric. Buried in the churchyard of the Temple Church.

GREAT FIRE OF LONDON (1666). See introduction.

GREAT PLAGUE. An epidemic of the plague, which started in the area around St Giles-in-the-Field and ravaged England from 1664 to early 1666, killing more than 75,000 out of an estimated population of 460,000.

GRESHAM, Sir Thomas (circa 1519-79). Merchant financier and founder of the Royal Exchange. He was the son of Sir Richard Gresham (Lord Mayor 1537) who was financier to King Henry VIII. Sir Thomas was educated at Gonville & Caius College, Cambridge, and obtained his B.A. at the age of 16. At the age of 24 he was elected a Freeman of the Mercers' Company. In 1559 he was appointed ambassador to the Netherlands. He died in 1579 and was buried in St Helen. He left his house and other property to found Gresham College, now part of the City University.

GREY, Lady Jane (1537-54). Great granddaughter of Henry VII, and titular Protestant Queen of England for 9 days in 1553. Beautiful and intelligent, she allowed herself to be put on the throne by unscrupulous politicians. After much heart searching, Roman Catholic Mary Tudor agreed to her execution.

GUILD CHURCH. A church that no longer has any parish duties and is free to follow a specialised ministry.

HARRIS, Renatus (René) (1652-1724). Born in France, an English organ builder whose fine instruments were highly regarded.

HATCHMENT. Square or lozenge shaped tablet, exhibiting the armorial bearings of a deceased person.

HAWKSMOOR, Nicholas (1661-1736). Born in Nottinghamshire. He went to London and worked for Sir Christopher Wren, where he stayed until Wren's retirement in 1718. He also worked in association with Sir John Vanbrugh in the building of Blenheim Palace, and at Castle Howard. Hawksmoor built 6 churches in the City after 1712.

HOLBEIN, Hans the Elder (born 1465, Augsburg Germany, died 1524). German painter associated with the Augsburg School, senior member of a family of painters.

HOLBEIN, Hans the Younger (born 1497, Augsburg Germany, died 1543). Painter, draughtsman and designer, renowned for the compelling realism of his paintings.

HOGARTH, William (1679-1764). English painter and engraver. Famous for his portraits and moralising genre scenes.

JONES, Inigo (1573-1652). Architect and theatrical designer, born in London. He was the son of a Smithfield clothworker. He studied architecture in Italy, where he was much influenced by the works of Andrea Palladio. He worked for King James I (1603-1625). His masterpiece was the Banqueting House at Whitehall. The Queen's House at Greenwich is another of his great works. In the last years of his life he worked for the Earl of Pembroke, rebuilding Wilton House. He died in Somerset House in 1652.

KEATS, John (Born in London 1795, in 1821 he died in Rome). English romantic poet. He produced work of great promise and quality before dying at the age of 25.

KNIGHTS TEMPLARS. Military order of monks, founded for the defence of pilgrims to Jerusalem in 1118. The power and wealth that they amassed caused envy which led to the order being discredited and finally disbanded in 1314.

LAUD, William (1573-1644). Archbishop of Canterbury in 1633. Son of a clothier, born in Reading. Educated at Reading Grammar School, before going up to Oxford. He became Dean of Gloucester in 1615, in 1621 Bishop of St David's, in 1627 Bishop of Bath and Wells (which he never visited) and in 1629 Bishop of London. Religious adviser to King Charles I. His persecution of the Puritans and other dissidents resulted in a show trial and execution by decree of a Puritan House of Commons.

LIVERY COMPANIES. Descended from the medieval guilds, various craft and trade associations within the City of London. Certain members were privileged to wear special clothing or "livery". Most were incorporated by Royal Charter between the 14th and 17th centuries. The Weavers' Charter dates from the 12th century. Most of the companies are governed by a self-appointing body known as the Court of Assistants, presided over by a Master or Prime Warden.

LLOYD'S OF LONDON. In 1688 Edward Lloyd kept a coffee house in Tower Street, and in 1692, in Lombard Street. Merchants and bankers met there to transact business informally, from which today's insurance market evolved.

MAGNA CARTA (1215). The barons, discontented with King John's extortion, forced him to sign the Great Charter, guaranteeing their rights and liberties.

MANSION HOUSE. The first official home of the Lord Mayor. Part of the site was in the churchyard of St Mary Woolchurch Haw. George Dance the Elder was chosen as the architect. The building, which cost £70,000, was built between 1739 and 1752.

MAYPOLE. A high pole painted with spiral stripes of different colours, and decorated with flowers and ribbons. It was set in an open space for revellers to dance around on May-day. Made of birch wood in the country but of harder wood in London, where it was left out all year.

MERCHANT TAYLORS' SCHOOL. Founded in 1560/61 by the Merchant Taylors' Company, a livery company of craftsmen tailors.

MILTON, John (1608-1674). The great epic poet. Born in the City of London.

MONASTERIES, Dissolution of. Thomas Cromwell was appointed Vicar General of ecclesiastical matters in 1535. He ordered a survey of all religious houses, and it was found that many had fallen into evil ways. In 1536, Parliament approved the suppression of all religious houses whose annual value was less than £200. Finally, in 1539, there was a complete authorisation that all religious establishments should be disbanded. The Crown obtained vast amounts of treasures and lands. Most of the lands were sold to members of the nobility.

MOORE, Henry (1898-1986). English sculptor of the 20th century. Identified with the 20th century trend towards "open form".

MORRIS DANCE. This pantomime dance has been known since the Middle Ages. It is of Moorish origin.

PEASANTS' REVOLT (1381). Oppressed workers rose against cruel exploitation and marched on London. Their leader, Wat Tyler, was pulled from his horse and stabbed to death at Smithfield. Brave intervention by the young Richard II (1377-1399) saved further bloodshed.

PEPYS, Samuel (1633-1703). English naval administrator and author of the greatest diary in the English language.

PINDER, Sir Paul (1566-1650). Ambassador to Turkey 1611-1620. He lived in a fine house at Bishopsgate, the facade of which can now be seen in the Victoria & Albert Museum.

RALEIGH, Sir Walter (1552-1618). Born in Devon. He was an adventurer and fought as a volunteer in the Huguenot army in two battles against Spain. In 1578 he joined with Humphrey Gilbert on an expedition to the Azores and the West Indies. In 1583-9 he funded six expeditions at a cost of £40,000. These were total failures; the only results were the introduction of potatoes and tobacco into England. King James I had him tried for high treason, convicted and condemned to be executed. Reprieved, he was imprisoned for 13 years in the Tower. He was released in 1616 in order to go on an expedition to El Dorado. The condition was that if he failed he would return. The expedition was a disastrous failure. True to his promise he returned. King James had him executed.

REFORMATION. The religious revolution that took place in the western church in the 16th century. Notable among the leaders of the revolution were Martin Luther and John Calvin. This was the beginning of the Protestant faith.

REREDOS. A screen or wall decoration at the back of an altar.

ROOD. Cross.

ROYAL EXCHANGE. From the early 16th century, there were plans to provide the City with a proper exchange building. Both Sir Richard Gresham and his son, Thomas, supported the idea. In 1567, funded entirely by Sir Thomas Gresham, the Royal Exchange was built on Cornhill. It was burnt down in the Great Fire of 1666. The second building was designed by the City Surveyor, Edward Jarman. It was completed in 1669. This building was also destroyed by fire in 1838. The present building, designed by Sir William Tite, was opened by Queen Victoria in 1844. It ceased to be an exchange in 1939. The building is now occupied by the Guardian Royal Exchange Assurance Company. The courtyard is used for exhibitions. Outside, the steps are one of the places from which a new sovereign is proclaimed.

SANCTUARY, Right of. A holy place, church or shrine, where protection or refuge could be sought. Some of these places were so venerated that even after the church had been destroyed, the ground where it had stood was inviolate.

SCOTT, Sir George Gilbert (1811-1878). An eminent Victorian church architect, known also for the Albert Memorial and St Pancras Station.

SMIRKE, Robert (1780-1867). The most successful architect (Greek revivalist), of the Regency period. His success was due more to the fact that he was an astute businessman, than to his style. He is mostly remembered for his design of the British Museum.

SOUNDING BOARD. A board or screen placed over or behind a pulpit, to reflect the speaker's voice towards the congregation.

SPENSER, Edmund (1552-99. Poet, born in London and educated at Cambridge. He entered into service with the Earl of Leicester before becoming secretary to the Lord Deputy in Ireland. He died in London and is buried in Westminster Abbey.

STOW, John (1525-1605). Elizabethan antiquary and author of the famous Survey of London 1598; revised and enlarged in 1603.

TOC H. A movement founded by the Reverend Philip "Tubby" Clayton (1885-1972), to practise a Christian way of life. This organisation brings together and helps all kinds of disadvantaged people. There are over 400 branches.

TOLERATION ACT, 1692. An Act granting freedom of religious worship on special conditions to Dissenting Protestants.

VANBRUGH, Sir John (1664-1726). Born in London, partly Flemish, the son of a rich sugar-baker. He was commissioned in the Earl of Huntingdon's regiment when he was 22. In 1690-2 he was imprisoned in the Bastille as a suspected spy and spent his time writing plays. He became an architect without any professional training and designed Castle Howard for his patron the Earl of Carlisle in 1699. In 1705 he was commissioned to build Blenheim Palace for the Duke of Marlborough. Vanbrugh was knighted by King George I in 1715 and the following year he succeeded Sir Christopher Wren as Surveyor of Greenwich.

WARDROBE. A building where all the Kings ancient robes of state and robes worn at special festivals were kept. The Wardrobe was burnt in the Great Fire. Upon the death of Ralph, Duke of Montague, the Master of the Wardrobe, in 1709, the office was abolished.

WHITTINGTON, Sir Richard (Dick) (died 1423). English merchant who became Lord Mayor for three terms. His history of success from rags to riches became legendary in stories, and later in pantomime. Son of a Gloucestershire knight, he opened a mercer's shop in the City, where he supplied the King and Court with costly materials. By 1400, he had amassed wealth and gained prestige. He lent money to Henry IV. (1399-1413), and Henry V (1413-1422). On his death he bequeathed his fortune to charitable causes.

de WORDE, Wynkyn (original name JAN VAN WYNKYN) (died 1534/35). An Alsatian born printer and astute business man who worked for William Caxton. He took over the business in 1491. First printer in England to use italic.

WORSHIPFUL COMPANIES. See Livery Companies.

WREN, Sir Christopher (1632-1723). Architect, designer, astronomer and geometrician. The greatest English architect of his time. He designed 53 London churches, including St Paul's Cathedral, and many secular buildings of note. A founder of the Royal Society and President 1680-82.

BIBLIOGRAPHY

Barker, F and Jackson, P. London. 2000 years of a City and its people. (London 1974).

Brooke, Christopher, and Keir Gillian. London 800-1216. The Shaping of a City. (London 1975).

Hibbert, Christopher. London the biography of a city. (London 1969).

Hobhouse, H. Lost London. A century of demolition and decay. (London 1971).

Hughes, M V. The City Saints. (London 1932).

Loftie, W J. London City, its history, streets, traffic, buildings and people. (London 1891).

London, Encyclopaedia of: Edited by William Kent, revised by Godfrey Thompson. (London 1970).

Ogilby & Morgan. Map of London Index. (London 1677).

Reynolds H. Churches of the City of London. (London 1922).

Rude, George. Hanoverian London 1714-1808. (London 1971).

Sheppard, Francis. London 1808-1870. The Infernal Wen.(London 1971).

Shepherd, T. London in the nineteenth century. Reprint of the 1829 edition. (London 1970).

Stow, John. A Survey of London (2 vols). Reprinted from the text of 1603 with intro. and notes by Charles Lethbridge Kingsford. (Oxford 1971)

Weinreb B, and Hibbert Christopher, (Ed). The London Encyclopaedia. (London 1983).

Alphabetical list of the Churches.

List of Demolished or Destroyed Churches.

All Hallows, Bread Street.	Demolished 1876.
All Hallows the Less Upper, Thames Street.	Destroyed in Great Fire.
All Hallows, Honey Lane.	Destroyed in Great Fire.
All Hallows, Lombard Street.	Demolished 1937.
All Hallows Staining. Tower remains.	Demolished 1870.
All Hallows The Great, Thames Street.	Demolished 1894.
Christ Church, King Edward Street. Tower remains.	Destroyed in Blitz.
Holy Trinity, Gough Square.	Demolished 1908.
Holy Trinity the Less, Trinity Lane.	Destroyed in Blitz.
St Alban, Wood Street. Tower remains.	Destroyed in Blitz.
St Alphage, London Wall.	Demolished 1923.
St Andrew Hubbard, Eastcheape.	Destroyed in Great Fire.
St Anne, Blackfriars.	Destroyed in Great Fire.
St Antholin, Watling Street.	Demolished 1874.
St Augustine, Watling Street.	Destroyed in Blitz.
St Bartholomew by the Exchange.	Demolished 1840-41.
St Benet Fink, Finch Lane.	Demolished 1842-44.
St Benet Gracechurch.	Demolished 1867.
St Benet Sherehog, Pancras Lane.	Destroyed in Great Fire.
St Botolph, Billingsgate.	Destroyed in Great Fire
St Christopher le Stocks. Under the Bank of England.	Demoloshed 1781.
St Dionis Backchurch, Lime Street.	Demolished 1878.
St Dunstan in the East. Tower remains.	Destroyed in Blitz.
St Ewine, Newgate.	Destroyed 1547.
St Faith under St Paul's.	Destroyed in Great Fire.
St Gabriel Fenchurch.	Destroyed in Great Fire.
St George, Botolph Lane.	Demolished 1904.
St Gregory by St Pauls.	Destroyed in Great Fire.
St James, Duke Place, Aldgate.	Destroyed in Great Fire.
St John the Baptist, Walbrook.	Demolished 1874.
St John the Evangelist, Friday Street.	Destroyed in Great Fire.
St John Zachary,Gresham Street.	Destroyed in Great Fire.
St Katherine Coleman, St Katherine's Row.	Demolished 1925.
St Lawrence Pountney, St Lawrence Pountney Lane.	Destroyed in Great Fire.
St Leonard Eastcheape.	Destroyed in Great Fire.
St Leonard, Foster Lane.	Destroyed in Great Fire.
St Margaret Moses, Friday Street.	Destroyed in Great Fire.
St Martin le Grand.	Destroyed 1548.

St Margaret, New Fish Street.	Destroyed in Great Fire.
St Martin Orgar, Martin Lane. Tower remains.	Destroyed in Great Fire.
St Martin Outwich, Threadneedle/Bishopsgate.	Demolished 1874
St Martin Pomeroy, Ironmonger Lane.	Destroyed in Great Fire.
St Martin Vintry, Queen Street,	Destroyed in Great Fire.
St Mary the Virgin Aldermanbury. Now in U.S.A.	Badly damaged in Blitz.
St Mary Axe.	Demolished before 1561.
St Mary Bothaw, Cannon Street Station.	Destroyed in Great Fire.
St Mary Colechurch, Old Jewry.	Destroyed in Great Fire.
St Mary Magdalen, Milk Street.	Destroyed in Great Fire.
St Mary Madgalen, Old Fish Street.	Demolished 1886.
St Mary Mounthaw.	Destroyed in Great Fire.
St Mary Somerset. Tower remains.	Demolished 1871.
St Mary Staining.	Destroyed in Great Fire.
St Mary Woodchurch Haw.	Destroyed in Great Fire.
St Matthew, Friday Street.	Demolished 1884.
St Michael Bassishaw.	Demolished 1897.
St Michael Crooked Lane.	Demolished 1831.
St Michael le Querne.	Destroyed in Great Fire.
St Michael Queenhithe.	Demolished 1894.
St Mildred, Bread Street.	Destroyed.
St Mildred in the Poultry.	Demolished 1872.
St Nicholas Acons.	Destroyed in Great Fire.
St Nicholas Shambles.	Destroyed 1587.
St Nicholas Olave.	Destroyed in Great Fire.
St Olave Jewry. Tower remains.	Demolished 1888.
St Olave, Silver Street.	Destroyed in Great Fire.
St Pancras, Soper Street.	Destroyed in Great Fire.
St Peter Cheape.	Destroyed in Great Fire.
St Paul's Wharf.	Destroyed in Great Fire.
St Peter Poor.	Demolished 1896.
St Stephen, Coleman Street.	Destroyed in Blitz.
St Swithin, Cannon Street.	Destroyed in Blitz.
St Thomas in the Rolls.	Destroyed in Great Fire.
St Thomas the Apostle.	Destroyed in Great Fire.